LOVE

JAMES P. GILLS, M.D.

CREATION
HOUSE

LOVE by James P. Gills, M.D.
Published by Creation House
Charisma Media Company
600 Rinehart Road
Lake Mary, Florida 32746
www.charismamedia.com

Unless otherwise noted, Scripture quotations are from the King James Version of the Bible. Used by permission.

Scripture quotations marked NASB are from the New American Standard Bible. Copyright © 1960, 1962, 1963, 1968, 1971, 1972, 1973, 1975, 1977 by the Lockman Foundation. Used by permission.

Scripture quotations marked AMP are from the Amplified Bible. Old Testament copyright © 1965, 1987 by the Zondervan Corporation. The Amplified New Testament copyright © 1954, 1958, 1987 by the Lockman Foundation. Used by permission.

Scripture quotations marked NIV are from the Holy Bible, New International Version. Copyright © 1973, 1978, 1984, International Bible Society. Used by permission of Zondervan Publishing House. All rights reserved.

Scripture quotations marked NKJV are from the New King James Version of the Bible. Copyright © 1979, 1980, 1982 by Thomas Nelson, Inc., publishers. Used by permission.

Cover design by Terry Clifton

Copyright © 2007 by James P. Gills, M.D.
All rights reserved.
Library of Congress Control Number: 2007931865
International Standard Book Number: 978-1-59979-235-4
E-Book ISBN: 978-1-61638-731-0

15 16 17 18 19 — 9 8 7 6 5 4
Printed in the United States of America

To Shea and Pit,

> Our two special children,
> And to Shane and Joy,
> Our son- and daughter-in-law.
> And to our grandchildren.
> May you all learn to express the height and
> depth of genuine love...better than I.
> With deepest affection and *storge* (appreciation),
>
> —Your dad

ACKNOWLEDGMENTS

All praise goes to the Lord of love,

Who teaches us daily

To love others as He loves us.

*Love is a medicine for the sickness of the world;
a prescription often given, too rarely taken.*[1]
—Dr. Karl Menninger

*The great tragedy of life is not that men
perish, but that they cease to love.*[2]
—W. Somerset Maugham

CONTENTS

*I believe in the sun even when it is not shining.
I believe in love even when not feeling it. I
believe in God even when God is silent.*[3]

—INSCRIPTION ON THE WALL OF A JEWISH HIDEOUT

COLOGNE, GERMANY

WORLD WAR II

*What's so remarkable about "love at first sight"?
What is truly remarkable is when people who have
been looking at each other for years enjoy an ever-
deepening expression of their love for each other.*[4]

—SAM LEVINSON

PROLOGUE

ONE STEAMY JUNE DAY IN 1962 IN SOUTH GEORGIA, a sixty-year-old Baptist minister with a pudgy frame and slow manner of speech peered at me quizzically over his glasses. "Son, why do you want to get married?" he asked bluntly. "What a stupid question!" I thought. In my youthful arrogance, I searched for a fitting response, but mental visions of a beautiful, red-haired woman thrust aside any semblance of sanity. I could hardly wait for the charming Heather Rodgers to become my wife. She also anticipated that magical moment when I would become her husband.

After an uneasy hesitation, I shrugged my shoulders and stated what I thought should have been the obvious. "We want to get married because...because we're in love."

He waited a few seconds and then asked softly, "What do you mean by *love*, Jim?"

He had me with that one. I shifted uncomfortably in my chair. The awkward silence between us grew, but he wouldn't let me off the hook. Finally, trying to sound casual, I broke the silence: "You know what I mean. We're just in love."

The kind pastor did not act the least bit surprised. He'd heard the same flimsy reason for getting married many times over the years. He just smiled and proceeded to give me a few pointers. Since I'd been taught to respect my elders, I listened politely—as much as my impatience would allow.

In the years since my marriage to Heather, I have contemplated love often, though regrettably I have *practiced* it far less. From what I see happening around me, it appears I'm not alone in my struggles. The songwriter poignantly described the need of our society: "What the World Needs Now Is Love."[1]

Half of the marriages in the United States will end in a state of absolute *un*-love. It's called divorce. Divorce is a destructive scourge in our society that scars individuals' souls for life. Now it is even possible for children to divorce their parents! How many people claim to understand love? And how many of those who comprehend it know how to practice it effectively? My concept of loving my wife when we were first married did not go beyond romance. That is not a criterion for a happy marriage. Married love has to become more than romance to be able to successfully face the crises of life that test it.

If love makes the world go 'round, then it's past time for us to discover what real love is. In this book, we'll examine some biblical principles that govern true love, which will help us to understand the essence of it. What is love? What makes it grow healthy and strong in relationships? Love for God. Love for others, especially in our marriage. What kills love? Together, we will probe for answers to these potentially life-changing questions.

Why the search?

So that we can love truly and experience the fulfillment and satisfaction that only true love offers.

PART ONE

LOVE AS WE KNOW IT:
AN OVERVIEW

There is no greater invitation to love than in loving first.[1]
—St. Augustine

Love seeketh not itself to please, nor for itself
hath any care, but for another gives its ease,
and builds a Heaven in Hell's despair.[2]
—William Blake

I have found the paradox, that if you love until it
hurts, there can be no more hurt, only more love.[3]

—Mother Teresa of Calcutta

His love…enableth me to call every country
my country, and every man my brother.[4]
—Daniel Wheeler

Faith is the key to fit the door of hope, but there
is no power anywhere like love for turning it.[5]
—Elaine Emans

Love is the art of hearts, and heart of arts.[6]
—Philip James Bailey

Love is like a beautiful flower which I may not touch but whose fragrance makes the garden a place of delight just the same.[7]
—HELEN KELLER

When we are in love we seem to ourselves quite different from what we were before.[8]
—BLAISE PASCAL

This heartwarming ad appeared in the classified section of a dignified metropolitan paper:

"I am responsible for all debts and obligations of my wife, Julia, both present and future, and am delighted to be the provider for a woman who has borne me two fine children, listened patiently to all my gripes, and with an overabundance of love and care made the past fifteen years of my life the happiest I have known. On this our fifteenth wedding anniversary, I am proud to express my gratitude publicly."[9]

Commitment gives substance to love.[10]
—HEATHER GILLS

Take away love and our earth is a tomb.[11]
—ROBERT BROWNING

I believe that every human mind feels pleasure in doing good to another.[12]
—THOMAS JEFFERSON

Love As We Know It: An Overview

AT THE RIPE OLD AGE OF TWELVE, I FELL IN LOVE WITH A very attractive young lady who lived down the street from me. How I adored that girl! She was so pretty, and I sure liked kissing her. I didn't even mind getting my buckteeth caught in her braces during those delightful moments. At that age, our relationship fulfilled everything I really wanted out of love. She made me feel good, which did wonders for my ever-expanding, fragile, male ego.

But what was I really saying when I whispered, "I love you," to my pre-teen girlfriend? Did I understand loving another person? No. I was actually making these bold statements: "I love myself. I just want you to help me do it."

We all make similar statements, to a lesser or greater degree, as we begin to pursue love and romance. Many of our first expressions of romantic love (too often shaped by the sales-conscious media) probably resemble what I experienced in my first puppy love. They are based in our own need, our desire to feel good about ourselves. While that may be an appropriate learning process, we must realize that in order to experience real love as mature adults we have to undergo a dramatic paradigm shift from attempting to fulfill our selfish needs to developing a desire to meet the needs of another. In short, to enjoy true love, we have to grow up and leave our skate keys and teddy bears behind.

My purpose in writing this book is to study a subject that I want to better understand personally—love. Becoming more deeply involved in the study of love will help each of us to experience more fulfilling dimensions of love. As we look at some of the hindrances to love, like selfishness, fear, and pride (hubris), we can evaluate our lives and determine to rid ourselves of these destructive attitudes. It seems to me that learning to love is a lifetime pursuit of greatest importance.

5

Children engage in lots of fuzzy thinking and speaking. We excuse their lack of rationale in the name of immaturity. But what about adults? To what do we attribute our obstacle where love is concerned? For example, we use the same four-letter word to describe the way we feel about a vast assortment of objects. I love my wife. I love my children. I love my dog. I love my profession. I love ice cream. I love windsurfing. I love…Just fill in the blank. Then, in the next breath, we exclaim, "I love God, and He loves me!" No wonder we're confused! How can we use the same word to describe our desire for ice cream as we do for our relationship with God?

Characteristics of Love

The ancient Greeks were more specific in their articulation of love. They used different words to describe different kinds of love: *epithumia, eros, philia, storge,* and *agape.* As we briefly define these characteristics of love, we can begin to evaluate our relationships more accurately, applying these character-istics to our objects of love as well.

Epithumia is defined as "desire, earnest desire, impulse, and most often, as lust." It is an intense longing, especially for what is forbidden.[13] In the Bible, it is used thirty-one out of thirty-eight times as "lust or evil desire for a forbidden thing." While it can be used in a positive sense for a strong desire for good (see Luke 22:15), it is not applied often in that way. Uncontrolled epithumia, when a strong desire for the forbidden, devastates individuals and society.

To Aristotle it meant groping for unlawful pleasure.[14] The ancient Stoics generally defined *epithumia* as a "desire after forbidden delight that defied all reason." The Bible warns against such a passionate desire for gratification: "Let not sin therefore reign in your mortal body, that you should obey it in the lusts [epithumia] thereof" (Romans 6:12). The apostle James explained clearly the spiritual consequences of yielding to forbidden desires of the appetites, saying, "Then when desire [epithumia] has conceived, it gives birth to sin; and sin, when it is full-grown, brings forth death" (James 1:15, NKJV).

When a man chooses the lawless, emotional lifestyle that epithumia involves, immersing himself in a world of forbidden, perverted pleasures, he ceases to be aware of God. Lustful desire can exert so much power over men's minds that they do outrageous and shameful things to themselves and to others. Modern psychology calls this slavery to inordinate pleasure an addiction; the "love object" consumes and controls the epithumia addict. The end of epithumia, according to the Scriptures, is death. Even for the Greeks, epithumia represented only the base, perverted, unreasonable desire for some object. To a person of integrity, such inordinate desire could hardly qualify as a desirable form of love, which the other Greek words express.

Eros is passionate love, with sensual desire and longing for romantic love.[15] It may be the most familiar word to many in the list of the five Greek terms for love. Sensual, erotic messages abound these days in every form of media and entertainment. One can hardly miss the countless advertisements that exploit the passions of human nature. It is possible that for some, sadly, eros is the only word for love to which they relate. Please don't misunderstand. Romantic infatuation can be a beautiful experience. Think back to that first crush you had as a youth. No matter how many years have passed since that memory, you will probably still enjoy the feelings of that "first love."

Do you remember how you felt when you saw that person or even just thought about him or her? A warm "rush" inside moved you in a way very little else could. Fresh and pure, lofty and noble, eros can stir us to new heights of love. Without eros, none of us would have been conceived. And few of us care to live without it.

The Scriptures approve of our desire for passionate love in the context of marriage: "Marriage is honourable in all, and the bed undefiled" (Hebrews 13:4). Eros holds a special place in a married couple's life together, as the Song of Solomon teaches clearly. In this poetic book of the Bible, the mutual love expressed so tenderly between the shepherd and his new wife teaches us not to scorn but to appreciate romantic passion in marriage. How could we despise such a beautiful gift that God has given us in marriage? His Word tells us that "every good and perfect gift is from above" (James 1:17, NIV). However, it is important to understand that the Scriptures also condemn eros outside of marriage as fornication or adultery. (See Hebrews 13:4.)

The Song of Solomon presents a beautiful picture of the uniting of physical, emotional, and spiritual bonds within a marriage relationship. This loving couple sets a biblical example for us to follow. In our marriage relationship, we need to understand that we can achieve a beautiful union of the physical and spiritual during intimate moments. Consider this time with your spouse as a celebration of life. I believe God would be delighted for us to thank Him for our spouse and worship together during our times of intimacy. To do so would add a whole new dimension of love within our marriage relationships. We should express radical gratitude to God for our spouse, as well as to our spouse for the love and life we share.

Philia is the Greek word that describes the love for a friend. Have you ever wondered how Philadelphia acquired the nickname "City of Brotherly Love"? It is based in this Greek word, not necessarily in the character of its inhabitants. Philia refers to friendship—the warm affection between girlfriends, buddies, pals, comrades, chums. The Greek root, *philos,* occurs twenty-nine times in the New Testament, all of which translate as "friend."[16] Amazingly, the word is even attributed to God's love or fondness for man: "But after that the kindness and love [philia] of God our Savior appeared...he saved us" (Titus 3:4–5).[17]

Philia does not have any connotation of eros passion. We may consider eros as a private passion between two people that God intended to be expressed in marriage. In contrast, philia refers to public friendship, which may occur between any two or more people. Developed over time, philia can be a tremendous blessing to those involved in friendship.

One of the better-known examples of philia in the Scriptures is that which blossomed in the friendship between Jonathan and David. Jonathan, the son of Saul, Israel's first king, became friends with David, the one who would take Jonathan's rightful place on the throne and become Israel's greatest king. They grew to love one another as brothers:

> And it came to pass, when he had made an end of speaking unto Saul, that the soul of Jonathan was knit with the soul of David...Then Jonathan and David made a covenant, because he loved him as his own soul.
>
> —1 Samuel 18: 1, 3

James, in his New Testament epistle, gives a word of caution to believers concerning friendships. Not every opportunity to develop such closeness benefits a Christian. Some friendships hinder our relationship with God. People following the world's ungodly philosophies have different priorities from those who strive to follow Jesus. James 4:4 states that friendship with the world means enmity (animosity, hostility) against God. That doesn't mean that Christians should walk around with their noses up in the air, unwilling to befriend those around us. We're here to minister to lost souls and to lend a helping hand to them. But we're not to get ensnared in any friendship relationship that presses ungodly priorities over Christian principles, which would place us at odds with God.

Storge (pronounced *stor-gay*) can best be described as affection, especially as it applies to good, old-fashioned love of family.[18] It is perhaps described best in the context of the almost indestructible bond between parents and their children, which overcomes terrible obstacles. You know, the blood-is-thicker-than-water kind of love. It endures for a lifetime. Where this type of love abounds, a unique freedom exists to experience life together, with all its joys and sorrows. We will discuss later in the text how storge applies as well to the most ordinary affections we have for our old, comfortable shoes, ice-cream, familiar surroundings, and other, more casual objects.

Many times we learn the lessons of life more by living than we do through any studies we may pursue. A loving family environment helps us to understand life. Godly parents must teach children sound biblical principles of right and wrong to prepare them to survive the difficult lessons of life. Yet, it is their storge affection that keeps them from burdening or oppressing the young into bondage of rules and do's and don'ts. Like a mother eagle with her brood of eaglets, storge also encourages children to test their wings. It doesn't isolate them from the reality of life. And if after all the teaching of godly principles they still yearn to set out on an opposing course, parental storge allows them that freedom when they have come of age and can fend for themselves.

The parable of the prodigal son, found in the fifteenth chapter of Luke, illustrates storge at its finest. When the son demanded his share of the inheritance, the father gave it to him. With a heavy heart (and what father's heart wouldn't be heavy?), he allowed his son to leave home to pursue his own agenda. When the son returned home, defeated, we see the beauty of a family enduring one of life's bitter lessons. They suffered from the son's wayward days, but in the end storge triumphed through forgiveness. The father's precious son was restored to his house. What better illustration could the Lord have used to depict our heavenly Father's love for all returning prodigals?

> And the son said unto him, Father, I have sinned against heaven, and in thy sight, and am no more worthy to be called thy son. But the father said to his servants, Bring forth the best robe, and put it on him; and put a ring on his hand, and shoes on his feet...For this my son was dead and is alive again.
>
> —Luke 15:21–22, 24

Agape is the most profound type of love, characterized by total commitment or self-sacrifice. It involves a willingness to give love to all, both friend and enemy.[19] In that regard, agape applies most accurately to the love of God. God alone specializes in agape, a devotion that gives whatever is best for others without thought of self-gain. However, it is also used biblically to refer to our love for others, even our enemies.

And, in the negative sense, agape was used in the Scriptures to describe one who had such a strong love for the world that he had forsaken the love of God. The apostle Paul wrote: "For Demas hath forsaken me, having loved [*agapao*] this present world..." (2 Timothy 4:10).

In human relationships, agape love involves a sacrificial commitment of oneself without yielding to a "what's in it for me?" attitude. Agape is a love that always acts in the best interest of the other person. The Christian, by God's grace and mercy, is required to love people whom he may not necessarily like or love in the sense of having warm, fuzzy emotional feelings toward them. Jesus taught that we must even love our enemies (Matthew 5:44). Thus, the Christian is required to always do what is good and have the best interest, even of his enemies, in mind when he or she acts.

In the book of Exodus, we read of God's commission to Moses when He spoke to him from the burning bush. Israel had cried for deliverance from Egyptian slavery, and their cry stirred God's heart of compassion. Moving in accordance with prophetic timing, God sent Moses to deliver Israel. Did the people want him? Not a chance. They were happy to be freed from Egypt, but when Moses led them into the wilderness, they became unhappy and murmured against him. They yearned for an immediate, miraculous entrance into their promised land. But God, in His loving wisdom, knew they needed to have their hearts tested.

Our own wants and needs don't always line up with God's purposes either, do they? The Scriptures declare that God is love (1 John 4:8). He knows the end from the beginning. Because He is always looking out for our best interest, in His love He gives us what each situation of our lives requires—nothing more; nothing less. Agape love does that. It is concerned for the best interest of another, without thought of the personal sacrifice required to fulfill that need. After overcoming his sense of inadequacy, Moses responded to God's call with agape love, without thought of the personal cost to himself, even in the face of strong criticism from the people he was to deliver.

Several thousand years later, the Jews were once again crying out for someone to liberate them from oppression, this time because of the cruelty of the Romans. In the fullness of time, God the Father again sent a deliverer to Israel: the Christ child. Yet Jesus didn't fit the description of the king Israel had in mind. He came to pay the full penalty for sin so that we could know complete deliverance and freedom. His selfless sacrifice is the ultimate example of agape love. He humbled Himself to become man and then died as a common criminal to restore us to right relationship with God and with each other. Through His death and resurrection, which cost Him everything, He became God's provision for our salvation. He came to restore all of mankind, including the Roman oppressors, to fellowship with God. In spite of the Jews' faulty concept of their deliverer, God's agape love allowed Jesus to be just who He was.

This brief overview of the different kinds of love should open our minds to wonderful possibilities for improving our relationships. Before we investigate them more closely, we will mention a few of the hindrances to experiencing and practicing love to its fullest that we all face.

As we consider love at its worst, we will confront our selfishness—our addiction to self, which distorts our personal pursuit of love. When we pursue love to get our selfish needs met, it ends in disaster. Pride (hubris), fear, and worry reflect our selfishness and work negatively in our lives, becoming strong enemies to our experiencing the reality of love. Understanding how to overcome these enemies will enable us to experience true love in ever greater dimensions.

Finally, we will consider love at its finest. We will zoom in on the one element that will help us experience our highest goal of perfected love: commitment. One of the most profound ways to be delivered from our internal enemies of love is through commitment. There are dimensions of true love that we can never know until we commit our lives to Christ. When we bow our knees to our Lord Jesus Christ and humbly ask for Him to transform our thinking and rid us of the enemies of His eternal love, His agape invades our lives.

God's commitment to us (John 3:16), our commitment to God, and then our commitment to loving others releases love—in every dimension—into our lives. It is simply a fact that without commitment, we will never experience the reality of love.

When you get right down to it, commitment represents the ultimate form of selflessness. It makes us willing and able to sacrifice for another. A strong foundation of commitment must be laid before the wedding vows if we expect them to be upheld after the honeymoon.

Commitment is foreign to the playboy who gets engaged and still goes out on his fiancée. Compare that irresponsible mindset to a young woman in our neighborhood who felt she had discovered the man God wanted her to marry. Without any great fanfare, she quit dating others. During their courtship, she supported and encouraged him, and after marriage, her commitment to God and to him remained unshakable. Even though he had some setbacks, she never allowed anyone to ridicule him. She helped make him into the very best of men because she committed herself to the relationship with her husband as the man God had sent to her.

I remember growing up with dreams of a special someone to love so I could find fulfillment as a man. Yet it came as somewhat of a surprise to me that to fulfill that desire I would have to commit myself to one woman and eliminate all my other options. I learned that, by a contract ordained in heaven, that woman was to be special both to God and to me. It was my lack of grasping God's revelation in the Bible and the lack of understanding of commitment in relationship that confused me. As a young man, I really needed to know God.

God gives Himself to us through Christ. We must commit ourselves to Him in humble faith. This is the pattern of commitment that we must copy in marriage. God's commitment is strong toward the believer. We live on His commitment to us, but we must learn throughout our Christian life to grow in our commitment to God. As we do, the rest of our desires fall into place. If we intellectualize, humanize, and rationalize our way out of commitment to anyone but ourselves, we are not living out our calling to be a channel of God's love to others. If we seek significance through our profession as a doctor, lawyer, teacher or whatever, we will suffer in every area of life. Our significance and satisfaction in life must come from receiving God's love and commitment to us and then growing in our commitment and love to Him.

We may think we can keep Jesus at a safe distance, but He will not settle for this. He calls us to divine intimacy through whole-hearted personal commitment. When we embrace this calling and respond in repentance and faith, we will find that all along God has planned for us what we were seeking. All our efforts at finding ourselves and our special niche in life can keep us from enjoying what we need most—an intimate relationship of mutual commitment with Jesus, the Son of God. This commitment will fill our lives with the revelation of His love, presence, and help.

We will begin to enter the romance, mystery, and joy of surrendering ourselves to God's grace, becoming enthralled with Him now and forever. In this framework of commitment to Christ, we will experience His love more and more. And we shall love more because of it. The apostle John wrote that "we love him because He first loved us" (1 John 4:19).

As you read this book, focus on these two words: *selfishness* and *commitment*. These powerful realities of life represent the ultimate of negative and positive perspectives of love. They will determine how we relate to God and to others and ultimately determine how fulfilling our love relationships will become.

Selfishness and commitment, respectively, reflect opposite ends of the spectrum of the human experience of love. Yet, both are a result of our choices and will have a staggering influence in every relationship. If we desire to know fulfillment in love, we must choose to walk in personal commitment to God and to the people we love. That is the only way to rid ourselves of selfishness so that we can enjoy the fullness of love that God intended.

As we make honest choices to know real love, we will have to face ourselves at our worst. Only then can God begin to change us and reveal the reality of love that He wants us to experience. Because God is love, He alone can define love at its finest for us.

PART TWO

HINDRANCES TO LOVE:
SELFISHNESS, PRIDE, WORRY

The highest holiness is the deepest humility.[1]
—ANDREW MURRAY

A fine wedding and the marriage license do not make the marriage; it is the union of two hearts that welds husband and wife together.[2]
—AUTHOR UNKNOWN

There is a Love always over you, which you may reject but cannot alienate; there is a Friend always with you who, even in your loneliest moments, leaves you not alone…that Love, that Friend, is God in Christ.[3]
—AMES DECKER HOLCOMB

To love is to admire with the heart: to admire is to love with the mind.[4]
—T. GAUTIER

Respect is what we owe; love, what we give.[5]
—PHILIP JAMES BAILEY

BECAUSE LOVE IS THE GREAT QUEST OF EVERY HUMAN heart, it is important to understand what keeps us from loving and being loved. Psychologists have many complex ideas of why certain individuals with particular backgrounds, traumas, and emotional responses cannot feel loved or learn to express love to others. Medical approaches can help people, but not without a definite decision on a person's part to make some changes in his or her perspective of life.

It is our basic human nature that creates the greatest hindrances to experiencing love. As we gain perspective of life as God ordained it, we can begin to see why our way of thinking hinders love to such a degree. Consider how the following attitudes may be hindering you from knowing true love.

Selfishness

Perhaps our greatest enemy to experiencing all aspects of love is our love of self. Selfishness is defined as being "concerned excessively or exclusively with oneself; seeking or concentrating on one's own advantage, pleasure, or well-being without regard for others."[6] None of us ever attends a "school of selfishness," yet even as newborn babies we demonstrate great skill in this area, and without effort, I might add!

Jean Piaget, a well-known child development specialist, explains the natural growth process of the infant. He refers to the cycle of selfishness, which he says surfaces at the mother's breast.[7] As infants develop through childhood into adulthood, ideally they become less dependent and more responsible, less demanding and more giving. The little boy who thinks only of taking what he wants should mature into the father who gives; the self-absorbed little girl should blossom into a nurturing mother.

Yet, this ideal maturation process is not always realized. Young ladies who grow up to be conscious only of their charm and beauty often feel they can make demands on relationships with young men. They select a husband based on his ability to meet these demands, and they seem to get most of what they want from him. Then, a surprise arrives—first baby! This new addition requires the young mother to change from her self-centered ways to the selflessness required in giving to her child for two o'clock in the morning feedings, diaper changes, and runny noses. Rather than being waited upon, this young mother must be available at all times to meet the needs of the child.

Not all mothers are able to readily accept the new demands of their infant. Some young women have become so accustomed to getting all the attention themselves that they cannot stand being out of the limelight. When they look into the mirror to see exhaustion peering back at them and note that their expensive and provocative mini-gown has baby's burps on the front of it, daydreams of romance turn into nightmares of the reality of motherhood.

These self-centered young mothers never learned how to give to others and so were unprepared for the rigors of a woman's most noble sacrifice of love: childbearing. The challenge to forsake their selfishness and embrace selflessness is indeed difficult, even unbearable, for some ladies. It is a medical fact that fatigue levels are greatest among women during their first years after having a baby. The dramatic changes in life that motherhood brings demand a healthy mind and outlook on life, which their selfishness does not give them. Of course, the tiny recipient of her sacrificial early-morning feeding never notices her pink satin boudoir slippers. The cycle has come full circle as the perfumed, pampered young woman becomes a baby-scented, pampering mother.

Others find motherhood the most fulfilling time in their lives, as they overflow with the maturing love of a mother. A closeness beyond all boundaries unites a woman with her baby, who is dependent upon her for its survival, and who will always be "her child." She gave of herself to bring a new life into the world and is grateful for the opportunity. No amount of giving would ever be considered a sacrifice. This maturing mother is learning a profound lesson in selflessness—commitment that characterizes love.

Similarly, some young men, absorbed in their toys and sports involvements, as well as body-building and other personal pursuits, enter into marriage and discover their own surprises. Marriage, as we mentioned earlier, is not all romance with the beautiful bride they courted. It involves the disciplines of daily employment, comforting a weepy mother-to-be, and paying the bills. Learning to give their time and energies to building a secure home and family circumvents many of their favorite activities, which is difficult for young men who were "born to play."

To some extent, customs, laws, and cultural pressure do curb a selfish attitude of "I want, therefore I'll take." But unless a radical spiritual transformation occurs, we'll never mature to the point of adopting the motto: I live, therefore I give. Human nature, even when motivated by good intentions, cannot produce perfect agape, self-sacrificial love based in commitment.

A Greek word that describes this radical transformation is *metanoia*: a radical change in thinking.[8] It's related to another word most of us are familiar with: *metamorphosis*, the type of transformation that turns a caterpillar into a butterfly. It means more than just a slight departure from the usual way of looking at things. *Metanoia* involves a drastic, about-face type of change in thought and attitude, a radical paradigm shift. It is the biblical word translated as "repentance," which involves a turning away from an accustomed way of thinking, which will be reflected in a change of behavior.

One of the main needs for such a radical change lies in the insidious nature of selfishness. Selfish love—which is really addiction to self—is cunning and deceitful. Selfishness would rather join forces with one of the other aspects of love to pervert its essential goodness than to stand alone. Selfishness acts like a cancer to true love. We usually see it stirring its ugly head under the guise of self-preservation. "Self-addiction" can grow in its influence in a life to such an extent that a person will dedicate his or her entire existence to a struggle for recognition and self-realization.

The world system glamorizes taking care of self first. Yet, whenever we focus our goals on personal achievements, acquiring affluent living conditions and seeking physical satisfaction, we destroy all hope of ever experiencing the meaningful fulfillment of love. Shallow, immature, Madison Avenue-style love barely skims the surface of the deep cry of every human heart to know love as God intended.

Even when we become aware of agape, most of us find it an impossible task to produce such unselfish love. Our consuming love of self prohibits our surrendering completely to God's love. Without that total commitment, we cannot know the will of God in relationships. We might be able to fool one another for a time, and even convince ourselves that we've got everything under control; but sooner or later our selfish nature prevails. Up it springs, if not in the same area we are trying to transform, then in another.

Marriage does not do away with the danger of self-centeredness. It simply exposes the truth of our motivation. Young people often jump into marriage for what they can enjoy rather than what they can contribute. What a setup for disaster!

In his book, *Charity and Its Fruits*, Jonathan Edwards, an influential pastor and prolific writer of the eighteenth century, described the nature of self-love as the result of Adam's sin. Adam and Eve's disobedience to God resulted in what theologians refer to as the fall of mankind from God's intended purpose. Their love relationship with God was destroyed. Edwards explains the devastating and far-reaching results of that loss. His language may sound a little archaic, but his observations and imagery remain quite contemporary:

> The ruin that the fall brought upon the soul of man consists very much in his losing the nobler and more benevolent principles of his nature, and falling wholly under the power and government of self-love…Before, his soul was under the government of that noble principle of divine love, whereby it was enlarged to the comprehension of all his fellow-creatures and their welfare…But so soon as he had transgressed against God, these nobler principles were immediately lost, and all this excellent enlargedness of man's soul was gone; and thenceforward he himself shrank, as it were, into a little space, circumscribed and closely shut up within itself, to the exclusion of all things else.[9]

The result of living a selfish life is to be "closely shut up" within ourselves, as Edwards expressed it. Love enlarges our world and allows for full expression of our souls—to God and to others. Later, as we investigate selfishness up-close (see Part Four), we will be able to evaluate our love-responses to see where we need a radical metanoia in our thinking. First, let's examine another powerful hindrance to experiencing the fulfillment love produces.

Pride: Hubris (Gk.)

It could be argued that the root of selfishness, in all its insidious opposition to true love, is pride. The Greek word for pride is *hubris*. In classical Greek ethical and religious thought, hubris (also spelled *hybris*) refers to "arrogant and exaggerated presumption, suggesting impious disregard of the limits governing human action in an orderly universe." Greek tragedies usually depict hubris as the hero's tragic flaw, even to the insistence of not needing the help of their deities. Even today, it is the sin to which the great and gifted are most susceptible.[10]

The seriousness of an individual indulging hubris is seen in today's diagnoses of sociopathic or psychopathic personalities. These people have a distorted sense of social and moral obligations, leading them to pursue immediate personal gratification in criminal acts, drug addiction, or sexual perversion.[11] They lose all sense of the reality of who they are and who people around them are as well.

The influence of pride upon the soul keeps a person from sensing any need of God. They think they know how to live life and what to think about every situation and person involved in their life. In their arrogance, they perceive people as objects to be used as a means to their ends, goals, and purposes. Even emotional desires are to be met, they think, by taking from spouses and friends what they perceive as their needs and rights. This exaggerated sense of self-worth is the epitome of selfishness.

Ellen Vaughn, in her wonderful book, *Radical Gratitude*, describes pride as a "crusty habit of focusing on ourselves rather than God."[12] She describes what pride looks like today:

> ...old-fashioned pride goes by all kinds of other names today. Self-sufficiency. Lifestyle rights. Autonomy. Modern American culture celebrates independence; after all, we are a nation of rugged individualists, "self-made" men and women who've pulled ourselves up by our own bootstraps...Pride isolates people from one another and from God...It is mutually exclusive with gratitude, for cultivating a thankful heart is not about autonomy, self-sufficiency, and self-congratulation, but dependence and thanks to Another. Gratitude to God is the manifestation of the fact that we rely on Him and trust Him, whatever comes.[13]

There is no place for tenderhearted love and humble gratitude in the mind of hubris, or inflated pride. Indeed, there is not even an idea of true love for one who is living in arrogant pride. Neither is there peace—with God, with one's self, or with others. To live in peace, we have to live in humility; a humble attitude that recognizes we are finite creatures, formed by an infinite Creator. It is the Creator who established the needs of our psyche and knows best how they can be fulfilled. The apostle Paul urged all Christians to seek the humility of Jesus, their Savior, when he wrote:

> Let this mind be in you, which was also in Christ Jesus: Who, being in the form of God, thought it not robbery to be equal with God: But made himself of no reputation, and took upon him the form of a servant, and was made in the likeness of men: And being found in fashion as

a man, he humbled himself, and became obedient unto
death, even the death of the cross.

—Philippians 2:5–8

Here the mind is again targeted as the seat of pride,
which needs to experience a metanoia (transformation) in
order to become humble. It is in humility that we recognize
our need of God and of others and begin to experience true
love in rightly relating to them. We appreciate the worth of
others and do not esteem our needs and desires greater than
another's. As members of the human race, we are all needy
creatures, groping our way toward God and love (Acts 17:27),
seeking to satisfy our deepest yearnings. Instead of exhibiting
hubris, which refuses to acknowledge or even feel a need for
God's love and the love of others, our heart must begin to
pulsate with humble longings for a loving Savior. In Andrew
Murray's Christian literary classic, *Humility*, he writes:

> …the Christian life has suffered loss, because believers
> have not been distinctly guided to see that nothing is more
> natural and beautiful and blessed than to be nothing, so
> that God may be all. It has not been made clear that it is
> not sin that humbles us most, but grace. It is the soul, led
> through its sinfulness to be occupied with God in His
> wonderful glory as God, as Creator and Redeemer, that
> will truly take the lowest place before Him.[14]

Humility—freedom from pride—is attained as we recognize who we are in the sight of our glorious Savior and bow in
grateful worship before Him. Andrew Murray contends that a
humble man or woman is one who not only bows their heart
before God in prayer, but also demonstrates their humility in
loving people around them. "The insignificances of daily life
are the importances and the tests of eternity because they prove

what spirit really possesses us. It is in our most unguarded moments that we really show and see what we are. To know the humble man, to know how the humble man behaves, you must follow him in the common course of daily life."[15]

It is only as we choose to walk in humility that we begin to appreciate the smallest expressions of love from God and from those around us. Then we are able to recognize the pain of others and desire to make their lives better, if only by a smile. Radical love, like the self-sacrificing agape of our Savior, Jesus Christ, can only grow in the soil of humility; pride will choke out even the seed of love that has been planted in our hearts.

A humble heart is thankful for every good thing it receives. Gratitude to God and to others for loving us is an expression of that humility. Ellen Vaughn describes the power of gratitude to transform our lives:

> Hot gratitude melts our hard pride. Again, it is the means of remaining in Christ. This thanksgiving for who He is mingles with daily thanks for all good gifts, from breath in our lungs to asparagus in the spring-time. Relishing who God is and all He's given is the secret of remaining connected to Him—and also of sucking the marrow from every ordinary day.[16]

Hubris is intent on building up its own self at the expense of others. It insists on being "number one," winning the adulation of people, and convincing others of its superior greatness. To show a need for love of God or of others would be perceived as weakness in a proud heart. The modus operandi of pride is to be self-sufficient, in need of nothing. Unfortunately, that includes not needing love, which means denying the deepest need of every human heart. The Scriptures concur that the nature of pride keeps man from love: "The wicked, through the pride of his countenance, will not seek after God: God is not in all his thoughts" (Psalm 10:4). Because God is love, the proud person cuts himself off from the primary source of love when he refuses to seek relationship with God.

It is important to determine how much influence hubris has in your life and your relationships. Where you see it working, you must determine to exchange its destructive power for the redemptive power of humility—seeking God's grace to set you free to bow before Him in love and worship. As you seek to love God, His love will fill your heart for others as well, and you will bow in humble gratitude before Him for the wonderful life He has given you.

Worry

Fear and worry are equally as formidable a hindrance to love as selfishness and pride. Stress in our lives is caused many times by worry. Anxiety can destroy our relationship with God and other people. We know medically that we can worry ourselves to death. Yet, we can never worry ourselves into a longer, healthier, happier life filled with love and fulfillment.

Relationships suffer when a person worries over daily decisions, producing an uneasiness that causes them to become irritable, even to the point of suffering a panic attack. Worry about where you left your purse, who got the promotion instead of you, or how you are going to pay the medical bills—these are just a few examples of hundreds of life situations that you can worry about. Some workaholics are driven by worries about financial security.

Fear can have tangible effects on your health, as in producing hypertension. The immune system suffers under the stress created by worry. When the immune system is decreased, common colds can overcome it, and eventually, as it breaks down further, even devastating diseases. A fearful person is usually a negative person who is not fun to be around. Relationships suffer when we are not positive, trusting, loving, supportive, and appreciative.

In *Rx for Worry*, the book I wrote to help myself learn how to fight against worry, I discuss the antidote for fear and worry:

> Chronic worry creates destructive anxiety and stress in our lives. It destroys our relationship with God and other people. When we embrace the negative mind-set of worry, we accuse others, judge others, discourage others and try to control others. We're negative people who don't feel God's love and can't love others. But when we have a thankful spirit, God's peace and love fill our lives.[17]

An attitude of thanksgiving is one of the best medicines for the worry disease. I refer to it as a *thanksgiving frenzy* to the Lord. Renewing your mind and emotions with an enthusiastic exclamation of thanks to God for Who He is and all He does for you on a daily basis will transform your negative, worry mentality. As Ellen Vaughn expresses it:

> Gratitude unleashes the freedom to live content in the moment, rather than being anxious about the future or regretting the past. So one's focus is free to have not only a keener awareness of spiritual blessings, but the physical pleasures of every day things we can taste, touch, hear, see, smell...All good gifts come from God. Not to enjoy them is to be ungrateful.[18]

Developing a mental attitude of giving continual thanks to God permeates your thoughts with God's faithfulness. As you choose to be thankful and give yourself to a "frenzy of thanksgiving," you will enlarge your relationship with God, change your relationships with others, and even influence your attitude toward your vocation or employment.

Worry, like selfishness and pride, is a terrible hindrance to our experiencing love for God and others. To fulfill our deepest desire for love, we must gain a new perspective of life. We need a metanoia, a radical transformation in our thinking. By choosing to seek God in humility, to care for others in maturity, and to be free from worry through giving thanks to God, we can experience a transformation of our minds. These eternal choices will open our lives to experience dimensions of love that we did not know existed.

As we humble our hearts, admitting our need of God, His grace and love come to us. Gratitude and awe fill our hearts for this God of love who gives us all we need for life. In *Rx for Worry*, I compiled a list of Scripture verses that are helpful for specific life situations that could cause us to worry. Some of them are included in the Appendix of this book. Listen to the prayer of the apostle Paul as he gratefully contemplates the love of Christ:

> For this cause I bow my knees unto the Father of our Lord Jesus Christ...That Christ may dwell in your hearts by faith; that ye, being rooted and grounded in love, May be able to comprehend with all saints what is the breadth, and length, and depth, And height; and to know the love of Christ, which passeth knowledge.
> —Ephesians 3:14, 17–19

PART THREE

KINDS OF LOVE:
UNDERSTANDING
RELATIONSHIPS

*Love is a fruit in season at all times, and
within the reach of every hand.*[1]
—MOTHER TERESA OF CALCUTTA

*He that shuts love out, in turn shall be shut out from love,
and on her threshold lie, howling in outer darkness.*[2]
—ALFRED LORD TENNYSON

Love is the only weapon we need.[3]
—REV. H. R. L. SHEPPARD

All for love…and nothing for reward.[4]
—EDMUND SPENSER

*A successful marriage requires falling in love
many times, always with the same person.*[5]
—MIGNON MCLAUGLIN

Kinds of Love: Understanding Relationships

LOVE, ACCORDING TO THE SCRIPTURES, IS THE VERY ESSENCE of God. The Bible does not only say that God has love or even that He loves; it states clearly that He *is* love—agape (1 John 4:8). So it was love that created the universe, the Earth and all that is in it, including mankind. No wonder we crave love so deeply and on so many levels; we were created by love Himself.

The Bible also makes it clear that the only reason we have a capacity to love God is that He first loved us:

> Herein is love, not that we loved God, but that he loved us, and sent his Son to be the propitiation for our sins. We love him, because he first loved us.
>
> —1 John 4:10, 19

Not only were we created *by* love—God Himself—we were also created *for* love—for God's pleasure (Colossians 1:16; Revelation 4:11). God's purpose in creating mankind was to glorify His love by giving us an intimate relationship with Himself. Without that spiritual relationship with our Creator, we can never hope to find true fulfillment in love. The seventeenth century French physicist and philosopher, Blaise Pascal, understood that reality. He wrote:

> There is a God-shaped vacuum in the heart of every man which cannot be filled with any created thing, but only by God, the Creator made known through Jesus Christ.[6]

Agape love flows from God to all His creatures. It is up to us to respond to His divine love, in accordance with the greatest commandment: "You shall love the LORD your God with all your heart, with all your soul, and with all your mind. This is the first and great commandment. And the second is like it: You shall love your neighbor as yourself" (Matthew 22:37–39, NKJV). As we pursue relationship with God through Jesus Christ, our Savior, we take the first step toward satisfaction of our deepest need for love.

Probably no one considers himself or herself capable of expressing agape love consistently in every relationship. That self-sacrificing, humble, pure love that God expressed when He sent Jesus Christ to die for our sins is not natural to our human nature. Yet, even the three natural loves—storge, philia, and eros—need to be energized by agape if we are to experience them in their most noble aspects of relationship. It is clear that we need supernatural help to experience love in the way God intended.

Let's look at the different aspects of love in a little more depth. I hope we are all becoming life-long students of the subject of love and the practice of it! No one has done a better job of analyzing love than C. S. Lewis. In his wonderful book *The Four Loves*, Lewis explains that the source of all love is God. He contends that unless we begin to relate properly to God's agape love, which he calls *charity*, we will not be able to fully enjoy the three natural loves: storge (affection), philia (friendship), and eros ("falling in love").

Then he describes four elements inherent in each of these different kinds of love:

- Gift-love, which longs to serve

- Need-love, which cries to God from our poverty

- Need-pleasures, preceded by desire

- Pleasures of appreciation, the starting point of
  our whole experience of beauty[7]

According to Lewis, *gift-loves* are those loves implanted in us that resemble most the agape love of God. In creation, God revealed His gift-love, designing us and everything around us with incredible beauty and functional design. In providing for our salvation through His Son, Jesus Christ, God also revealed His gift-love to all of mankind. There is no good thing that does not represent the giving heart of our heavenly Father.

The caring of a husband and father for his family, which causes him to work and save money for their future when he is no longer here to benefit from it, is an example of gift-love. And, astonishing though it may seem, we can express gift-love to God in meaningful ways. When we show kindness to others, especially those who are not lovable, Jesus said it is as though we are doing it to Him personally:

> For I was an hungred, and ye gave me meat: I was thirsty, and ye gave me drink: I was a stranger, and ye took me in: Naked, and ye clothed me: I was sick, and ye visited me: I was in prison, and ye came unto me... And the King shall answer and say unto them, Verily I say unto you, Inasmuch as ye have done it unto one of the least of these my brethren, ye have done it unto me.
>
> —Matthew 25: 35–36, 40

Need-love is that which says of a woman, "I can't live without her." The craving to be loved is complicated. Without cultivating the nobler aspects of love, it can be selfishly indulged. Yet, need-love has a legitimate place in our lives. It is what causes a frightened child to run to its mother's arms.

No one calls a child selfish because it turns for comfort to its mother. It is need-love that best characterizes our human nature. We are born helpless, and as soon as we are fully conscious we discover loneliness; we need others physically, emotionally, intellectually.[8]

When we seek to know God's love, we are crying out from our need for forgiveness or for help in our troubles. As we humble ourselves to seek God, we become more aware of our incredible need for help in order to make sense of our lives, to untie things that are now knotted together, and tie up things that are still dangling loose. While our need of God never ends, we must take care not to lose our awareness of that need. If we do, our need-love will die with it.[9]

Need-pleasures are those pleasures preceded by desire. Satiating your thirst (need) with a cool glass of water brings a pleasurable response. You did not drink the water just for the pleasure of it, but because you needed it. If these need-pleasures get out of hand, as in overeating for the sheer pleasure of it (gluttony), they end in an unhealthy state of mind and body. Unhealthy personal absorption with your own needs ends in addiction, which is self-destructive.[10]

Pleasures of appreciation are described by Lewis as "that unexpected pleasure of enjoying a beautiful rainbow or an unexpected call from a friend." He uses the example of going for a walk and passing a beautiful garden when, suddenly, the fragrance of sweet peas fills your senses. They come so unexpectedly and so gratifyingly that they claim our appreciation by right. They give us the sense that we owe it to them to savor, attend, and praise them. Lewis says that appreciative pleasure is the beginning of our whole experience of beauty. For example, appreciation for creation leads us to the inevitable experience of appreciating the Creator.[11]

In summary, it is our *need*-love that cries to God from our poverty; our *gift*-love that longs to serve God and our *appreciative*-love that says: "We give thanks to thee for thy great glory."[12] As we live our lives from youth to old age, we continually discover different, age-related gift-loves, need-loves, and pleasures of appreciation. These elements of the natural loves will only assume a right balance in our lives as we submit ourselves to God's agape love—charity. Allowing His love to flow through our lives keeps us from unhealthy absorption with natural loves, giving them a godly quality that expresses itself through a godly character.

In Part One we defined the three natural loves: storge, philia, and eros. As we discuss each of these valid kinds of love in more depth, I encourage you to do as I have done and evaluate the place of each in your relationships. How can you improve their quality? Can you bring gift-love into relationships that have been based on need-love? Which relationships would be strengthened by adding storge, affection that can mingle itself with the other kinds of love? And are there ways to submit your relationships to agape love, God Himself, that will release greater fulfillment of natural loves? Do all of this with a renewed appreciation-love for God and others.

Storge (Affection)

Storge, according to C. S. Lewis, is the humblest of all the loves. Affection is modest and does not put on airs. While people can be proud of being in love (eros) or even of friendship (philia), storge lives humbly "in our most private things: soft slippers, old clothes, old jokes, the thump of a sleepy dog's tail on the kitchen floor."[13] Affection is a love itself. However it can also mingle with the other loves and "become the very medium in which from day to day they operate."[14]

In friendship, for example, storge appreciates the familiarity of the friend, their endearing ways, even their quirks that bring a smile. Affection for certain places where friends meet, their likes and dislikes, phrases they use, and facial expressions enhance the feeling of friendship. "Even in eros, there is a peculiar charm," says Lewis, "about those moments when Appreciative love lies, as it were, curled up asleep, and the mere ease and ordinariness of the relationship wraps us round. No need to talk. No need to make love. No needs at all except perhaps to stir the fire."[15]

As with all of the natural loves, unfortunately, there is a dark side of storge. If not energized by agape, mere affection based in need-love will demand more than it gives, craving the affection of others in an unreasonable way. The most unloving, unkind person expects to receive this broadest of the natural loves from family and friends. Without offering affection from the gift-love side of storge to others, he or she still craves their affection. Lewis says that "Affection produces happiness only if there is common sense, give-and-take and decency; that is, you need justice, continually stimulating mere Affection when it fades and restraining it when it forgets or would defy the art of love... [You need] goodness, patience, self-denial, humility, and the continual intervention of a far higher sort of love than Affection. If we try to live by Affection alone, Affection will 'go bad on us.'"[16]

Philia (Friendship)

Philia, friendship, is the least natural of the loves, according to C. S. Lewis. That is, friendship is not motivated by instinct, biological needs, or necessity. In short, we can survive without friendship, though it would not be a pleasant survival. Friends are chosen freely between individuals, with openness and sharing of mind and heart as the norm. In friendship, there is respect for individuality and an inclusive atmosphere that appreciates a person's intrinsic worth. Lewis describes friendship as that "luminous, tranquil, rational world of relationships freely chosen...Friendship is a relation between men at their highest level of individuality."[17] True friendship is not possessive or jealous. "Two friends delight to be joined by a third, and three by a fourth...In this, Friendship exhibits a glorious 'nearness by resemblance' to Heaven itself where the very multitude of the blessed (which no man can number) increases the fruition which each has of God."[18]

Friendship is a very precious kind of love. The Scriptures confirm the wonderful reality of friendship love. The Old Testament patriarch, Abraham, is called "the Friend of God" (James 2:23). Through his reverence for and obedience and loyalty to God, he cultivated that special relationship. And Jesus referred to friendship on several occasions, no more directly than in this passage:

> Greater love hath no man than this, that a man lay down his life for his friends. Ye are my friends, if ye do whatsoever I command you. Henceforth I call you not servants; for the servant knoweth not what his lord doeth: but I have called you friends; for all things that I have heard of my Father I have made known unto you.
> —John 15:13–15

According to the Scriptures, we can be friends of Jesus as we submit to His lordship in our lives. Friendship is a relationship between individuals where openness and sharing of mind and heart are the norm. Can you imagine an infinite God and Savior desiring to call us friends? Of course, we will never be equal with God. Yet, the agape love of God, given to us by grace, has "raised us up together…in heavenly places in Christ Jesus" (Ephesians 2:6). By choosing to obey His commands, we lay down our selfish "lordship" and allow Him to take His rightful place as Lord of our lives. And we enjoy a divine friendship relationship with God.

The love of God is also referred to in the Scriptures as friendship—*philanthropia*—on occasion: "But after that the kindness and *love* [philanthropia-Strong's #5363] of God our Savior toward men appeared…He saved us" (Titus 3:4–5). Only God can be perfect in friendship; we cannot. Yet, friendship bonds us to God and to others with ties of loyalty and respect. Jesus taught that friendship involves a willingness to sacrifice one's own life for a friend. We can do this in many small ways: giving up our momentary activity to help a friend, become a listening ear, offer an encouraging word. Selflessness is not only demonstrated through friendship in life and death matters; it is more often seen in everyday concerns of life. Offering a simple prayer for an anxious heart can be a "laying down of one's life" for the concern of a friend.

Eros ("Falling in Love")

Eros, according to Lewis, is "sexuality which develops within 'love'."[19] He writes, "The event of falling in love is of such a nature that we are right to reject as intolerable the idea that it should be transitory. To be in love is both to intend and to promise lifelong fidelity."[20]

In that context, it is eros that makes a man desire not just any woman, but a particular woman. And not to desire her for the pleasure she can give, but to desire her as the beloved, herself. This is sexual desire at its best, not focusing on ourselves, but on the beauty of the beloved. In contrast to sexual desire without eros, Lewis concludes, "one of the first things Eros does is to obliterate the distinction between giving and receiving."[21] Thus, the key to unselfish married love is to express the pleasures of appreciation-love in eros.

While eros is most often considered a need-love that says, "I can't live without you," the gift-love element of eros can strengthen and beautify marriage. Lewis writes, "Appreciative-love gazes and holds its breath and is silent, rejoices that such a wonder should exist even if not for him, will not be wholly dejected by losing her, would rather have it so than never to have seen her at all."[22] It is gift-love in eros that desires to give her all good things: permanence, fidelity, happiness, comfort, protection, and if possible, wealth.[23]

C. S. Lewis lists three reasons to consider seriously the demands of eros before contemplating marriage:

- First, theologically, because this is the body's share in marriage which, by God's choice is the mystical image of the union between God and man.

- Secondly, on the moral level, in view of the obligations involved and the incalculable momentousness of being a parent and ancestor.

- Thirdly, it has a great emotional seriousness in the minds of the participants.[24]

Lewis also warns that eros, as with the other natural loves, when "honoured without reservation and obeyed unconditionally, becomes a demon."[25] Not only are the lovers in danger of idolizing each other, but also of idolizing eros itself. The noble expression of eros in marriage can only survive, according to Lewis, when it is "continually chastened and corroborated by higher principles."[26]

Higher Principles

All of the natural loves, in order to be positive forces in our lives, must be infused with and motivated by higher principles of agape's self-sacrificing love. Jonathan Edwards understood the importance of these principles, which he expressed in his two hundred-page treatise, *Religious Affections*. He concluded that godly affections are more important than decisions of the mind because affections determine decisions. When we have true religious affections, we *desire* to obey the Ten Commandments. Our heart has been transformed and is filled with God's agape kind of love, which motivates us more powerfully to obey God's commands than a decision of an unregenerate mind. When affections are changed through a genuine change of heart, that inner resource dramatically transforms the expression of our life.[27]

In our relationship with God, according to Edwards, there is an exchange of hearts in love. We are refreshed and enlivened by the joy God possesses and the delight He shows in us. Though God's love is much greater than what we can offer Him, yet there is a sweetness in the tears of repentance and humility that we offer to Him in worship through the years. As we pour them out to our beloved Savior, our soul finds its satisfaction in God. We are renewed and healed and can live from the strength of that love. Edwards concluded that the nature of wholeness lies in union of the soul with God, as the branch is one with the vine (John 15:5).[28]

Thus, the natural loves—affection (storge), friendship (philia), and romantic love (eros) all need to be submitted to the higher principles of true, heart-changing religious affections found only in agape. Edwards declares that our love to others becomes an overflow of these godly affections and delight in God. He says, "If you start at the wrong place and do not seek love and satisfaction in God first, you will experience perpetual frustration, because no human being can bring this satisfaction. When God Himself is your first love and chief portion, then you find overflowing joy and love within to channel to others, independent of their appreciation. This is the new life!"[29]

From this sublime state of recognizing the divine possibilities of all the kinds of love we have discussed, we must descend for a while into the valley of lovelessness, where too many people dwell. In order to experience love at its best, we must learn to recognize love at its worst. Then we can make intelligent choices to upgrade our love experiences by applying the principles we are learning about love.

PART FOUR

LOVE AT ITS WORST:
SELFISHNESS UP CLOSE

Selfishness separates from heaven; sacrificial generosity heightens our joy in it.[1]

—JOHN PIPER

Love is the master key which opens the gates of happiness.[2]

—OLIVER WENDELL HOLMES

Love is the only force capable of transforming an enemy into a friend.[3]

—MARTIN LUTHER KING, JR.

There is no remedy for love but to love more.[4]

—HENRY DAVID THOREAU

Love is space and time measured by the heart.[5]

—MARCEL PROUST (1871–1922)

Love feels no burden, thinks nothing of trouble, attempts what is above its strength, pleads no excuse of impossibility; for it thinks all things lawful for itself, and all things possible.[6]

—THOMAS A KEMPIS

He who lives only for himself is truly dead to others.[7]

—PUBLILIUS SYRUS

The need for devotion to something outside ourselves is even more profound than the need for companionship. If we are not to go to pieces or wither away, we must have some purpose in life; for no man can live for himself alone.[8]

—Ross Parmenter

You will find as you look back upon your life that the moments when you have really lived are the moments when you have done things in the spirit of love.[9]

—Henry Drummond, British Clergyman

Discipline puts back in its place that something in us which should serve but wants to rule.[10]

—A. Carthusian

Some pray to marry the man they love, my prayers will somewhat vary; I humbly pray to Heaven above that I love the man I marry.[11]

—Rose Stokes

The level of lust parallels the level of selfishness. The level of commitment parallels the level of love.[12]

—Jim Gills

A loving heart is the truest wisdom.[13]

—Charles Dickens

The loneliest place in the world is the human heart when love is absent.[14]

—E. C. McKenzie

*Love begins when a person feels another person's
needs are as important as his own.*[15]

—HARRY STACK SULLIVAN

*Love and pity and wish well to every soul in the
world; dwell in love, and then you dwell in God.*[16]

—WILLIAM LAW

*That you may have pleasure in everything, seek
your own pleasure in nothing. That you may
know everything, seek to know nothing. That you
may be everything, Seek to be nothing.*[17]

—ST. JOHN OF THE CROSS

*When a man sees that a neighbor hates him, then he
must love him more than before to fill up the gap.*[18]

—RABBI RAFAEL

One forgives to the degree that one loves.[19]

—FRANÇOIS DE LA ROCHEFOUCAULD

*Love must be learned, and learned
again; there is no end to it.*[20]

—KATHERINE ANN PORTER

What is love? It is the morning and the evening star.[21]

—SINCLAIR LEWIS

Ten Steps to Carnal Living

1. Spend as much time watching secular television as you possibly can. You owe it to yourself!
2. Eat sweets often and give into every craving for food immediately.
3. Love yourself more, and God and others less.
4. Fill your life with fun things and avoid adversity at all cost.
5. Be a taker, not a giver; after all, you already pay taxes!
6. Never do anything that could be construed as fanaticism; you do have an image to uphold!
7. Don't worry about having daily devotions; you don't have time!
8. When you are confronted with sin in your life, go directly into delusion.
9. Anytime you have a problem, go straight to a psychology book; it knows much more about life than the Bible.
10. Give in to every sexual urge; after all, God created you with them.[22]

—STEVE GALLAGHER, PURE LIFE MINISTRIES

Could we forbear dispute, and practise love,
we should agree as angels do above.[23]

—EDMUND WALLER

To love as Jesus loves; that is not only the Lord's precept,
it is our vocation. When all is said and done, it is the
only thing we have to learn, for it is perfection.[24]

—RENÉ VOILLAUME

To love at all is to be vulnerable. Love anything and your heart will certainly be wrung and possibly be broken. If you want to make sure of keeping it intact, you must give your heart to no one, not even to an animal. Wrap it carefully round with hobbies and little luxuries; avoid all entanglements; bolt it up safe in the casket or coffin of your selfishness. But in that casket—safe, dark, motionless, airless—it will change. It will not be broken; it will become unbreakable, impenetrable, irredeemable... The only place outside Heaven where you can be perfectly safe from all the dangers of love... is Hell.[25]

—C. S. Lewis

Love gives itself; it is not bought.[26]

—Henry Wordsworth Longfellow

Love is a better teacher than duty.[27]

—Albert Einstein

Love is most nearly itself when here and now cease to matter.[28]

—T. S. Eliot

We only deliberately waste time with those we love—it is the purest sign that we love someone if we choose to spend time idly in their presence when we could be doing something more constructive.[29]

—Sheila Cassidy

The more thou thine own self
Out of thy self dost throw
The more will into thee
God with his Godhead flow.[30]

—ANGELUS SILESIUS

Death is not an end, but an event in life—indeed, a new
start for an extended knowledge and a purer love.[31]

—BISHOP OF LINCOLN

Love is energy of life.[32]

—ROBERT BROWNING

LOVE

GREECE SAID, "BE WISE—KNOW YOURSELF." ROME SAID, "Be strong—discipline yourself." Psychology says, "Be confident—assert yourself." Materialism says, "Be satisfied—please yourself." Religion says, "Be good—conform yourself."

I have tried much of this self-help advice over the years and it left me empty. Jesus said, "Deny yourself and follow Me" (Matthew 16:24).

I'm learning, one day at a time.

How do we become more concerned for others and less so for our own comfort? First, we have to unlearn what our cultural paradigm has taught us. Despite what the self-centered trend of current philosophies teach, we can survive (and thrive) without becoming addicted to self. The fact is that we will never truly thrive in the love quotient if we pursue the selfish, self-exalting philosophies of the day.

Ingrained selfish habits can so overwhelm us that victory over them seems an insurmountable task. We must strive to win the battle against selfishness. So much lies at stake—for us and for others. According to many experts in human behavior, selfishness stands alone as the most common mental illness. O. Quentin Hyder, M.D., supports this concept in his book, *A Christian's Handbook of Psychiatry*:

> Selfishness is the root cause of all sin, and the result of sin may sometimes lead to personality or adjustment problems and some neurotic, psychosomatic or even psychotic conditions.[33]

Of course, Dr. Hyder assures us that sin alone doesn't cause *all* mental breakdowns or emotional disturbances, but it plays a key role. If selfishness leads to mental illness, we could presume that selflessness—in an individual or a nation—leads to the soundest state of mind. To have the mind of Christ is to become selfless and to be filled with perfect love. It is important to remember for sound mental health, develop the desire to *give* rather than *take*.

In case we lack the motivation to conquer our oldest foe—selfishness—a short tour through history might provide the incentive. Ancient Rome, that vast and mighty civilization, fell prey to pagan enemies. First, though, it fell prey to the enemy within. The core rotted. Selfishness enjoyed a heyday. Leaders and followers alike cared more about their own narcissistic pleasure than anything else. We need only to look around at our own country to see many of the same tendencies. We're rushing down that path at breakneck speed. Without major changes, we may very well wind up suffering the same fate of internal collapse—or worse. I heard noted author and speaker Chuck Colson say, "The greatest crisis in America today is the crisis of character…no society has ever survived without a strong moral code." Sobering words, indeed.

Selfishness, like litter strewn beside a scenic highway, mars the landscape along the road to God's kind of love. It spoils the trip. A greater awareness of specific "me-isms" can help us detect the litter of selfishness and dispose of it. Do any of these habits sound familiar: worry, self-pity, manipulation, and greed, to name a few?

As an eye surgeon for over thirty years, I see similarities between selfishness and cataracts. While cataracts restrict physical sight, selfishness obstructs spiritual sight. I have had the privilege of removing many cloudy lenses and implanted brand new ones, enabling light to focus on the retina so people can see. The love of God can do the same for people who suffer from spiritual cataracts.

Spiritual cataracts darken our hearts and minds. They hinder the radiant light of Christ's love from shining through us to the world. It takes more than a phacoemulsifier machine to remove this stubborn spiritual kind of cataract—only the divine Physician has the necessary skill and tools to do that. If you're ready, let Him begin the examination.

Selfishness Goes to School

In Psalm 118:8 we read, "It is better to trust in the LORD than to put confidence in man." Humanism tries to transform selfishness into science. One of its basic tenets declares that we must love ourselves before we can love anyone else. Christians believe otherwise. Not only does humanism attempt to remove God from the love loop, it elevates man above God. In practical experience, the concept proves false.

People do not love others better by loving themselves more; they only grow into more proficient narcissists. Modern psychological theories and various other forms of counseling deviate from the teachings of Scripture. The faulty ideas of self-realization and "finding oneself" have attained popularity among humanists, but these goals reinforce selfishness and lead to the enthronement of personal works and accomplishments. In contrast, the Christian humbles himself to give glory to Jesus Christ in all his accomplishments.

We have seen in the greatest commandment (Matthew 22: 37–39) that the commands of Jesus absolutely violate the natural, inborn selfishness of mankind. John Piper, in his book *What Jesus Demands from the World,* discusses fifty commands that Jesus gave us to obey in order to live an unselfish life that "displays the worth of his person and the effect of his work."[34] Piper says that learning to depend on the life of Jesus in us to fulfill these commands leads to ultimate purpose. He explains, "When obedience to his commands happens, what the world sees is the fruit of Jesus' glorious work and the worth of his glorious person. In other words, they see the glory of God."[35]

Of course, we cannot fulfill these demands in our own personality or strength. Piper says that "the obedience he demands is the fruit of his *redeeming* work and the display of his *personal glory*. That is why [Jesus] came—to create a people who glorify his gracious reign by bearing the fruit of his kingdom" (Matthew 21:43).[36]

Piper understands that to be free from selfishness requires sacrifice. Yet, he is quick to point out that our acceptance with God is not based in our having a generous spirit first:

> Before we can be generous, God receives us into his favor through faith in Jesus (John 3:16). He takes us into his family as his children (John 1:12). He counts us righteous (Luke 18:14); he forgives our sins (Matthew 26:28); he gives us eternal life (John 5:24). None of these is obtained in this life by first overcoming our selfish spirit. It is the other way around. We recognize our selfish spirit and despair of overcoming it on our own and turn to Jesus as our only hope. In this turning to Jesus, we are justified, forgiven, adopted, secured in his care forever (John 10:28–30). On that basis we now make progress in overcoming our selfish spirit.[37]

Gratitude for all that God does for us through Christ to redeem us from our selfish, sinful nature inspires our love for God and motivates us to love others. In *Exceeding Gratitude for the Creator's Plan,* I explained:

Simply stated, eternal life is *knowing God*. To know Him involves properly appreciating who He is, who He made you to be, and all that He has given you for life. As we continually yield our lives to Christ, we can enjoy the quality of eternal life now, in this troubled world, which will prepare our hearts to live with God forever. These desirable qualities of eternal life are described in Scripture as peace, joy, righteousness, strength, and rest for our souls. Love, patience, perseverance, and every other named characteristic of God are worked in us as we yield our souls to His redemptive process.. [38]

Overcoming Selfishness

History reveals many saints who did indeed "yield their souls to His redemptive process," overcoming their selfish spirit through Christ's redemptive power. Many years ago, William Booth, founder of the Salvation Army, was preparing to send his annual Christmas message to his workers around the world. It had to be sent by telegraph and payment was required for every word. Money was in short supply, so William Booth sent a one-word message: *others*. This was the central focus of Christ's coming to earth to bring salvation to mankind, and it was the focal point of Booth's life and ministry.[39] In his profound Christmas message to his workers, he communicated his expectations of them as well.

Mother Teresa of Calcutta lived her life entirely for others. Her sacrificial generosity was not made for the rich and famous, but for the most humble, poverty-stricken, sick, and dying people she could find. She said, "Today, the poor are hungry for bread and rice and for love and the living world of God."[40] As she ministered to outcast lepers in India, she exemplified a "life for others." Those poor people could not help themselves, and could do nothing for her in return. What a high ideal she set! She fulfilled the command in Scripture, "Be kindly affectioned one to another with brotherly love; in honor preferring one another" (Romans 12:10). And she followed Christ's admonition: "For if ye love them which love you, what thank have ye?...And if ye do good to them which do good to you, what thank have ye? for sinners also do even the same....Be ye therefore merciful, as your Father also is merciful" (Luke 6:32–33, 36).

We must challenge ourselves to know whether we have a superficial experience of Christianity or an ever-growing relationship with the Lord of love. We may study the Word and attend spiritual retreats; we could even teach Sunday school and serve on church committees! But we may still have much to learn about surrender and obedience to Jesus' commands. We must ask, where is our burning desire to love and obey God? To love others? To love our enemies? It takes a growing vision of the beauty and glory of God to maintain a continually growing victory over selfishness. As we behold the Redeemer in worship and adoration, we are changed from glory to glory by the Spirit of God (2 Corinthians 3:18). We are continually changed to become more like Jesus. Cultivating these godly affections in the presence of God is the way to become selfless. It is then that we become obedient to the command: "in lowliness of mind let each esteem other better than themselves" (Philippians 2:3).

It is not so much our determination to change that changes us; it is our determination to worship the Lord Jesus and to live in His presence that brings effective change in us. As we learn to draw near to God, we find a greater desire to know Him, to love Him, and to obey His commands.

The satisfaction of experiencing the limitless love of God transforms our thinking. Out of this increasing communion with God flows a life dedicated to serving others. The Savior says, "He who abides in Me, and I in him, bears much fruit" (John 15:5, NKJV). He also said, "I am among you as he that serveth" (Luke 22:27). He is our pattern that we must allow to mold us. Experiencing His love for us is the catalyst that propels us to give our lives to serve others. We are simply to be channels of His love. We are to love others as He loves us. His love for us stirs up our love for Him and others. The love of Christ constrains us (2 Corinthians 5:14)!

I often fail to practice what I believe, but my affection for God makes me desire to practice it more perfectly. And I'm learning to trust the Lord instead of myself to make it happen. Even as a growing Christian, I still find myself torn between devotion to *me* and devotion to *Him*. The apostle Paul spoke of this human struggle: "For I have the desire to do what is good, but I cannot carry it out. For what I do is not the good I want to do; no, the evil I do not want to do— this I keep on doing" (Romans 7:18–19, NIV). Paul gives us the key to overcoming this struggle: "What a wretched man I am! Who will rescue me from this body of death? Thanks be to God—through Jesus Christ our Lord!" (Romans 7:24–25, NIV).

John Piper observes that sacrificial generosity is grounded in the goodness of God to us *before* and *while* we are generous to others. We are able to love and give because He has already given freely to us and promises to meet every need we have in a lifetime of generosity (Matthew 6:33; 7:7–12; Luke 12:32)."[41]

Step one for walking out of the pattern of selfishness is to accept the reality that God openly reveals Himself to us.

Step two is to open ourselves to God, bringing to Him our cares, our sins, and our open hearts poured out in transparency before Him. Step three follows, then, that after we have established a transparent relationship with God, we can freely open ourselves to others in loving relationships.

God opens Himself to us saying, "I AM THAT I AM" (Exodus 3:14). He reveals His love to us through the Scriptures and through His Son, Jesus. And as we surrender to the power of the Holy Spirit to transform our thinking (Romans 12:1–2), we will reflect the love of Christ more and more through the sacrificial generosity of our lives.

Jesus promises His rest for those who will come to Him and be open and transparent with Him. He said, "Come unto me, all ye that labour and are heavy laden, and I will give you rest. Take my yoke upon you, and learn of me; for I am meek and lowly in heart: and ye shall find rest unto your souls" (Matthew 11:28–29). The psalmist instructs us to "Cast thy burden upon the LORD, and he shall sustain thee" (Psalm 55:22). And the apostle Peter concurs: "Humble yourselves therefore under the mighty hand of God, that he may exalt you in due time: Casting all your care upon him; for he careth for you" (1 Peter 5:6–7). Such abandon to God's loving care will cause us to be transparent in His presence.

Again, the psalmist calls on us to "Trust in him at all times; ye people, pour out your heart before him" (Psalm 62:8). And the New Testament invites us to "confess our sins," for "he is faithful and just to forgive us our sins, and to cleanse us from all unrighteousness" (1 John 1:9).

The apostle Paul told the Corinthian church, "We have spoken freely to you, Corinthians, and opened wide our hearts to you. We are not withholding our affection from you, but you are withholding yours from us. As a fair exchange—

I speak as to my children—open wide your hearts also" (2 Corinthians 6:11–13, NIV). Paul demonstrated the necessity of opening our hearts and giving our affections to each other. James tells us to be open with each other even concerning our faults: "Confess your faults one to another, and pray one for another, that ye may be healed" (James 5:16).

The Scriptures point to Christ as our hope of overcoming the selfishness within our nature. His unselfish pattern of living will make us open and transparent, considering others' needs before our own. God's pattern of openness and transparency will serve us well in having an intimate, transparent, fulfilling relationship with one's spouse, as well as with family, friends, and in winning lost souls to Christ.

As we discussed, it is hubris (pride) that makes it difficult for us to be open with God and others. When we choose to humble ourselves before God, accepting the lordship of Christ in our lives and becoming transparent with Him, we will be able to be transparent with one another. We will risk being vulnerable. The apostle Paul told the Corinthian church, "So I will very gladly spend for you everything I have and expend myself as well. If I love you more, will you love me less? (2 Corinthians 12:15, NIV). It is clear that whether or not this church was going to reciprocate Paul's love he would humbly offer it, becoming vulnerable and giving his life to secure their faith in Christ. Paul sets a high standard, but it reflects the spirit of Jesus, which true believers are bound to emulate.

Those who choose to experience intimacy with Christ will find the joy of fellowship and communion with God. Then they will be able to be a channel of God's love to others. The rewards are great—in marriage, family, friendship, and winning souls to Christ. The cost is humility that results in honest transparency, trust, and vulnerability of our hearts before God and others.

It is a work of the Holy Spirit in our lives that will enable us to pursue this divine intimacy with God. As we become filled with God's grace, we can give ourselves to another as Jesus gave Himself to us, laying down His life for us. He admonishes us to "love one another; as I have loved you, that ye also love one another" (John 13:34). To do that, we must follow the pattern of the Master, who humbled himself to become a man and the servant of men. Then we will experience the love of God and be able to share it with others. His love will infuse all the natural loves that God has given for us to enjoy. We will be filled with godly affections that motivate us to love in every situation of life.

The What-Ifs Syndrome

We discussed worry as one of the hindrances to love. Have you considered the fact that worry is selfish. Why? Because it forces us to fixate on and fret about potential harm to self (or others important to self) and it negates faith in God's promises. Worry can devastate a person's health. Not only that, it can infect others close to us like a contagious disease. In *Dake's Annotated Reference Bible*, there is a list of eighteen characteristics of worry, the first cousin to self-pity. It is an outstanding list that should be considered prayerfully.

Worry is:

1. Sinful and produces fear.

2. A disease causing other ills.

3. Borrowing trouble that cannot be paid back.

4. Brooding over what may not happen.

5. Creating trouble, misery and death.

6. A burden borrowed from time or others.

7. Weight that kills prematurely.

8. Mental and physical suicide.

9. A gravedigger that has no sympathy.

10. Needless and wasted time and effort that should be spent constructively.

11. A robber of faith, peace, and trust in a never-failing heavenly Father.

12. A stumbling block to others.

13. A disgrace to God that should never be indulged in by Christians.

14. Anxiety over what is nothing today and what is less tomorrow, in view of faith.

15. Anticipating troubles which seldom come to those who trust God.

16. Torment over something that will likely be a blessing if it comes.

17. Living like an orphan without a heavenly Father.

18. A crime against God, man, nature, and better judgment. Jehovah Shalom is God's peace in righteousness.

—Dake's Annotated Reference Bible[42]

Whenever I waste time stewing about legal, family, or business matters, I wind up in an emotional cauldron. Worry reduces my effectiveness and restricts my capacity for love. I can't detect the needs of others around me while my thoughts churn away on personal concerns.

Does worry about others, especially our children, mean we love them more? Not at all. In fact, it means we are choosing to court sin. We can't justify worry if we view it in the light of God's Word (See Matthew 6:25–34, Luke 12:29, and Philippians 4:19.) Here is one of my favorite Scriptures that teaches us what to do with worry. I encourage you to memorize it:

> Be anxious for nothing, but in everything by prayer and supplication with thanksgiving let your requests be made known to God. And the peace of God, which surpasses all comprehension, will guard your hearts and your minds in Christ Jesus.
>
> —Philippians 4:6–7, NASB

Pity Parties Are for Kids

Self-pity ranks high on the selfishness scale. It grieves God. If you doubt that, turn to the book of Numbers and read the story of the Israelites who felt sorry for themselves while trekking through the wilderness. A poor-me attitude focuses on unfulfilled personal wants, leaving no room to thank God for His many blessings. (See 1 Timothy 6:6 and Philippians 4:11.)

There are sometimes legitimate feelings of self-concern. Even Jesus expressed these emotions in prayer when in His crisis in the Garden of Gethsemane the night before His crucifixion (Mark 14:32–36.). Yet, our complaints, in contrast to His, usually stem from ingratitude, worry, and self-condemnation more than a righteous cause.

The normal self-pity found in young children should diminish as they mature. Often, that doesn't happen. Children grow up physically, yet fail to attain any level of moral and spiritual maturity. As a result, they develop negative attitudes of ingratitude toward everything in life.

We've all known adults who forever whine about their circumstances. They complain about their deficient wardrobes, physical attributes, their mates, friends, houses, churches—even the weather. Approximately seventy-five percent of American workers dislike their jobs. Many employees are so discontent that they will criticize their job at length to anyone who will listen.

As a rule, people who wallow in self-pity live with unrealistic expectations of life. For example, some workers expect to receive higher wages without giving anything of value in exchange. Their negative attitude infects others around them, sapping their strength as well. A wise man of old wrote, "A merry heart doeth good like a medicine: but a broken spirit drieth the bones" (Proverbs 17:22).

I would venture to guess that most of us succumb to self-pity now and then. Some days I indulge myself when things don't go my way or I feel that associates don't cater to me enough. At the clinic, I sometimes have to repeat instructions over and over. I feel that no one listens to me. My throat gets sore from talking, and I start feeling sorry for myself, so my attitude takes a turn for the worse.

While I'm wallowing in my own mire of self-pity, I forget others' needs. For example, some patients, especially senior citizens, may simply have a hard time hearing me! They need help to receive instructions accurately. I've found a logical solution for the dilemma: I encourage my staff to share the responsibility of giving important instructions along with me. I practice focusing on the real need—that of the patient—instead of my perceived hardship.

The art of contentment takes time, but if we are to demonstrate God's love, we will expend the effort. Without whining. The apostle Paul taught us that we must *learn* to be content: "Not that I speak in respect of want: for I have learned, in whatsoever state I am, therewith to be content" (Philippians 4:11).

Losing the Blame Game

The awareness of wrongs we've committed in the past sometimes hangs over our heads like a heavy weight. Guilt gnaws on our innards like a swarm of termites on a piece of choice wood until we're left feeling hollow and worthless. We don't know quite when the load will drop and crush us.

When we suffer under a load of guilt, it is safe to say that we're not living in the grace of God. In that risky condition, we can never relax enough to simply love Him, others, or even life. But, oh, when we come to Jesus! God shows His deep love for us through the divine love-gift of forgiveness. One of His greatest blessings in our lives is that He releases us from the threatening burden of sin and guilt.

I remember the sense of relief that flooded my soul the day I accepted Jesus as Lord. I often see similar relief mirrored in others who have recently come to faith in Christ. His divine gift of peace outperforms any anti-depressant on the market. Jesus promised His followers: "Peace I leave with you, my peace I give unto you: not as the world giveth, give I unto you. Let not your heart be troubled, neither let it be afraid" (John 14:27).

The Holy Spirit does convict us of sin by making us recognize our guilt before God. That is not the same as the nagging feeling of self-condemnation called false guilt, which many people suffer. Godly conviction leads us to repentance, where we find His peace, while false guilt drives a wedge continually between us and Him.

For example, an adult who was molested as a child carries inside a "shame core" for a sin that is not his to claim. Or consider the many believers who ask for forgiveness over and over for the same sin because they harbor a sense of false guilt. That is the devil's tool to rob believers of the peace that God came to give (Romans 5:1; 8:1).

"Then how can guilt be considered selfish?" you might wonder. Consider this: clinging to guilt involves a decision to place self (personal ego/feelings) on the throne instead of faith in God's Word, which promises forgiveness and cleansing from all sin and guilt. We choose to carry those hurtful feelings instead of allowing the Holy Spirit to cleanse us and give us His peace. He says if we admit sin with a sincere heart, He will forgive. He will bind up our wounds. He will set us free (Luke 4:18). End of guilt, whether real or perceived! If we do not believe God's promise, we are pridefully saying, "I'd rather not confess to God or anyone else, thank you. I prefer to stay miserable in my sin or my sense of false guilt."

True contentment thrives only in the fertile hearts of those who know they have been forgiven by God. We need to ask for and receive forgiveness daily so we can forget the past and look forward to the joy of being with Him forever. Why wait until forever? Do it now. Believe the promise of God's Word: "If we confess our sins, he is faithful and just to forgive us our sins, and to cleanse us from all unrighteousness" (1 John 1:9).

The Greener-Grass Trap

According to Greek legend, a prominent athlete placed second in an important race. He brooded over his loss night and day. Envy of his rival consumed him—so much that he decided to destroy a large statue erected in the winner's honor. As he chopped away at its base, the statue fell on him and crushed him. What a lesson for us!

Envy is the sin of a selfish heart that wants what another has. Nothing can appease a selfish heart full of envy. If it cannot overtake the one envied on its own merits, it will surely try to rob the achievements, possessions, reputation, or blessings of that person. Things get out of hand when this vile emotion runs wild.

Many biblical accounts warn us of the destructive force of envy. The sibling rivalry between Cain and Abel festered and caused Cain to kill his brother. Joseph's jealous brothers desired to kill him. Instead, they seized the opportunity to sell him into foreign slavery. King Saul envied David to the point of madness and attempted murder. Even mature Christians who yield to more subtle expressions of envy lose their intimacy with God and others as a result of their sin. The Scriptures warn: "Let us not be desirous of vain glory, provoking one another, envying one another" (Galatians 5:26). "But put ye on the Lord Jesus Christ" (Romans 13:14).

Not-So-Wiser Misers

Selfish greed mixed with fear produces imbalance, improper evaluation, and poor decision-making. A quick glance at the stock market provides a good example of greed functioning in the business world. It is commonly accepted that greed can cause dramatic swings on Wall Street. Investors rush to buy huge amounts of a particular company's stock, forcing the price up. Then, fearful of incurring losses, they sell their shares and decrease the value significantly for everyone. This practice allows them to buy back at even lower prices. And the cycle of greed continues.

Jesus declared that we cannot serve two masters: God and money (Matthew 6:24). John Piper explains that the idea of serving here relates more to *worshiping* than to merely "providing a service." He says that the reason Jesus taught so much about money is that in all cultures and throughout history, it represents the alternative to God as the treasure of our hearts, and therefore the object of our worship:

> Serving money means looking to money to provide you a service and to provide your help and meet your needs. Serving money means planning and dreaming and strategizing and maneuvering to be in a position to maximize our wealth and what money can provide for us. Money is the giver and the benefactor in this servant-master relationship... You look to money to do good for you... So what Jesus is saying is that we should serve God... We look to God to be our helper, our benefactor and treasure. To serve him would be to

plan and dream and strategize and maneuver to be in a position to maximize our enjoyment of God and what he alone promises to be for us. God then, not money, becomes the giver and the benefactor in this servant-master relationship.[43]

Piper concludes that Jesus showed such remarkable concern with what we do with our money because of the basic principle He taught: "Where your treasure is, there your heart will be also" (Matthew 6:21). "In other words, the reason money is so crucial is that what we do with it signals where our heart is. 'Where our heart is' means where our worship is. When the heart is set on something, it values it, cherishes it, treasures it. That is what worship means."[44]

In relationships, the greed syndrome is also apparent. A greedy person, concerned only with immediate gratification, will buy into a relationship for what he or she can get out of it. Then, rather than becoming vulnerable enough to develop mutual trust and love, their fear of rejection (loss) forces a flight to their next quick-gain affair.

If we commit ourselves wholly to God, the selfishness of greed's destructive, fear-producing cycle will not plague us, either in business or in personal relationships. As we learn to rest in God's unconditional love, we can risk loving others. There is no greed or fear in love: "There is no fear in love; but perfect love casteth out fear" (1 John 4:18). God's love is our pattern of generosity: "For God so loved the world that he gave his only begotten Son" (John 3:16).

Domination Station

Do you know anyone suffering from eating disorders like bulimia or anorexia nervosa? For whatever emotional reasons, the victims of such disorders have a high need to control something in their lives, so they choose the most accessible thing—their bodies. Their drive for domination causes them to manipulate dietary habits to the point of self-destruction.

The same thing can happen in interpersonal relationships. Whether within the family, church, or business community, everyone suffers when we try to control others for our own selfish gain (while declaring we have only their best interest at heart). Even if we temporarily succeed in getting our way, bitterness takes root in those we try to dominate in this way. They may not even know why they feel animosity, but unconsciously they know they've been used. And they resent it.

A manipulator neither appreciates nor respects others. To him, people are objects to do with as he pleases. This controlling attitude is completely opposite to the ways of the gentle Holy Spirit, who delights in every creature and draws them to God with love, guiding them into truth.

Those who selfishly manipulate others worry most about being in charge and about who is calling the shots. Issues such as a sudden financial setback, loss of position, or fear of death create a special anxiety. Why? Because in all these situations we have zero control. One way to combat the desire for control in the area of finances is to become a good steward over what we have, give a generous portion of our income to charity, and commit the remainder to God.

To relinquish this unhealthy need to control, we need to humbly acknowledge that the Lord supplies everything we have in life—youthfulness, health, employment, possessions, and family. Someday, whether we want to or not, we must release it all to Him anyway. Choosing to do this now, in the name of the Lord, exemplifies the highest kind of humility and love. It allows us to become whole and free.

God's command comes with wonderful promise: "Trust in the Lord, and do good; so shalt thou dwell in the land, and verily thou shalt be fed. Delight thyself also in the Lord; and He shall give thee the desires of thine heart" (Psalm 37:4–5).

What's Yours Is Mine

In America, when a company catches an employee stealing (whether outright taking or defrauding through poor work habits), they will probably not retain that employee's services any longer. Trust has been broken and credibility destroyed.

Americans have occasionally watched national news and seen shocking looters taking advantage of victims' misfortune during life-threatening storms or riots. They walked into broken-down storefronts and homes to carry off whatever they desired.

In some cultures, people make ends meet, not by working hard, but by stealing. Once headed down such a path, they soon convince themselves of their dependence upon thievery to survive. These people get trapped into a deteriorating physical and moral ghetto. We read in Galatians 6:7–8:

> Be not deceived; God is not mocked: for whatsoever a man soweth, that shall he also reap. For he that soweth to his flesh shall of the flesh reap corruption; but he that soweth to the Spirit shall of the Spirit reap life everlasting.

The thief does not show love for God or his fellow man. But Jesus can transform his life from one of taking to one of giving. God is love, and love gives.

Story Hour

Lying is a selfish, destructive sin that permeates human nature. A young wife goes on a shopping spree and spends five hundred dollars. Knowing the family is tight for money, she tells her husband she spent only one hundred dollars. A new business in town expands quickly because the owner has a special knack with customers. His competitors try to destroy him by spreading rumors that he's on the verge of bankruptcy.

Advantages finagled through lies, either white or black, always result in reduced rewards in the end. This selfish habit, used to protect oneself or to destroy another's credibility by altering the truth, damages the perpetrator in the end. Once found out, credibility and trust are destroyed, and every future contact is tainted.

Love demands truthfulness, even if it hurts. Ephesians 4:15 says, "Let our lives lovingly express truth [in all things, speaking truly, dealing truly, living truly]" (AMP). Proverbs 18:21 reminds us, "Death and life are in the power of the tongue: and they that love it shall eat the fruit thereof."

Longing for Forbidden Fruit

From the moment we learn to reason until the time we die, we all struggle with some form of inordinate desire—lust. It is reflected in various forms: lust for food, possessions, power, fame, money, etc. And it is experienced to different degrees, from extreme desire to outright addiction. But when we see the word *lust*, our first thought probably relates to inordinate sexual desire, which is the counterfeit of marital love.

We do not have to actually commit an act of adultery in order to open the door to moral destruction. Mental adultery can be destructive as well. Sources of perverse, pornographically explicit materials are more readily accessed in our society than ever before. Yet, the fact is, they do not give the satisfaction they promise, but tear us away from the peace of God-directed love and unity in marriage. In place of a beautiful gift of marital love, lustful desires produce only frustration and exquisite loneliness.

Selfishness is the motivation for all sexual relationships outside the bonds of marriage. Giving in to such illicit desires inflicts painful wounds on the soul that remain long after the activity stops, and even if the partners marry. It is true that if they confess their sin, God will forgive them; but the painful consequences of a few moments of stolen pleasure can last a lifetime.

Lustful sexual desires can be conquered when we surrender our lives to God and choose to know the satisfaction that only comes through a life of commitment in marriage. Married couples living in harmony with the Lord's will are aware that they belong to God. All of His divine promises are theirs to enjoy in a life of commitment to their marriage relationship. As my devotion to both the Lord and Heather has grown, I have discovered the joy of committed love to Jesus and to my lovely wife.

God's way fulfills us; premarital or extramarital sex never will. Lustful sexual desires are never satisfied. They continually clamor for more. When we have God's best, who wants the rest? Overcoming mental lust, even within marriage, however, still requires commitment to God and repentance. I have found that developing a consistent prayer life with my wife helps remove these barriers to deeper intimacy with God and her.

"Let your fountain [of human life] be blessed [with the rewards of fidelity], and rejoice in the wife of your youth" (Proverbs 5:18, AMP).

Uppity Yuppities

Any time we look down on other people and focus only on their weak points, we reveal our own self-righteous pride. We use this technique for a purpose—to draw attention away from our inadequacy and insecurity. We feel it protects us from close scrutiny; yet, it also hinders intimate communication. All this to convince ourselves that we still reign at the center of our own little worlds. From such a lofty position of self-deception, we make unwise decisions that carry serious consequences. As it says in Proverbs 16:18, "Pride goeth before destruction, and an haughty spirit before a fall."

No Different Strokes for Different Folks

Our investment corporation, Jireh, employs two opposite types of people—accountants and developers. The developers do manage to get investments done, but the accountants don't appreciate their super-optimism one bit. They tend to believe what Arthur James Balfour said (with tongue in cheek): "It is unfortunate, considering enthusiasm moves the world, that so few enthusiasts can be trusted to speak the truth."[45] Not to be outdone, the developers show little patience for the methodical accountants' seeming inability to move on an idea.

Even though people with different personalities always have to work hard to appreciate and understand each other, we need the stability that results from each point of view in business and elsewhere. In church, the "doers" (developers, positive thinkers, enthusiasts) will try almost anything to become more effective for Jesus. The "thinkers" (accountants, planners, and realists) frown on these free spirits, who are less calculating than they. Yet, all the varied perspectives on life have their special niche in a Christ-centered program, balancing truth and progress.

I have seen churches where differing ideas flourish like wildflowers in a beautiful meadow. In other congregations, members stumble over mundane details, like what color the new carpet and choir robes should be. Selfish, petty differences lead to serious strife on a local and national scale. Disgruntled families leave a church and some churches even split apart because people refuse to appreciate each others' uniqueness and opinions. This lack of charity results in severe criticism within the church and toward the church, as outsiders witness the disarray.

Conflict inevitably arises in all kinds of relationships, whether within a large group or between two mates. Judson Edwards describes the problem well in his book *What They Never Told Us About How to Get Along With Each Other*. He describes relationships as collisions of different worlds; we just need to make them *tender collisions*.[46] Tender collisions bring to mind an image of a friendly round of bumper cars at the county fair—in contrast to a bad accident on the interstate. Which would you prefer? Of course, there is room for disagreement in relationships. But in healthy relationships, you decide to walk in love and let the final authority rest on the Word of God. As one wise man has said, "Choose to major in majors and minor in minors."

The apostle Paul admonishes us: "With all lowliness and meekness, with longsuffering forbearing one another in love, Endeavouring to keep the unity of the Spirit in the bond of peace" (Ephesians 4:2–3). The Greek word for "forbearing" can be translated as "tolerating, enduring, or putting up with."[47] It is a sad commentary that in our culture some segments of non-Christians practice tolerance more than some Christians. We are instructed in the Scriptures to strive for unity of the Spirit by learning to show tolerance for brothers and sisters who have different perspectives and opinions than we do.

Don't Confuse Me With Facts... My Mind Is Made Up

Unbelief could adopt that phrase as its slogan. In fact, unbelief is the epitome of a self-on-the-throne mentality. It prohibits mature, loving relationships with the Lord and with others. For the true skeptic, anything goes. Left to run wild, this tendency in our selfish natures will take over like the kudzu weed in Florida.

Marriage provides a hothouse environment for selfishness to multiply, except for the Lord's intervention. As a husband and wife each choose to leave self behind and move closer to God, they automatically grow closer to one another. (Think of a triangle with God at the top point and man and woman at each of the other two points.)

Pistis, the Greek word for "faith," means "conviction of the truth or belief respecting man's relationship to God and divine things; the conviction that God exists and is the

Creator and ruler of all things, the provider and bestower of eternal salvation through Christ."[48] Pistis must take root in a heart before the flower of genuine love can bloom. First John 4:7 teaches us: "For love is from God; and everyone who loves is born of God and knows God" (NASB).

Faith in God involves belief in who He is and what He says. By doubting the authenticity and authority of God's Word, we guarantee that the survival-of-the-fittest mentality will rule, not only the animal kingdom, but the human kingdom as well. Where that is the case, there will be no abundant joy that comes from living a life committed to the will of God.

Though an unbeliever's achievements sparkle by the world's standards, they cannot fool God any more than a cubic zirconium can fool a diamond specialist. The currency of the kingdom of God is love based in faith. The Bible warns: "Without faith it is impossible to please him: for he that cometh to God must believe that he is, and that he is a rewarder of them that diligently seek him" (Hebrews 11:6).

Assuming the Worst

Cynics, as Webster defines them, are "faultfinding, captious critics."[49] Having lost the ability to appreciate the good in life, they focus on the negative to the exclusion of the positive. They wear a complaining attitude like a trademark. H. L. Mencken said, "A cynic is a man who, when he smells flowers, looks around for a coffin."[50]

Due to their pessimistic outlook, cynics find it difficult to submit to God, and in turn, to love others. In the 1950s, cardiologists Meyer Friedman and Ray Roseman developed the theory that the behavior of chronically angry and impatient people raises their risk of heart attacks. They discovered that impatient individuals who walked and ate in a rush, interrupted others, and complained constantly were more likely to suffer heart problems. Friedman and Roseman labeled these caustic critics Type A personalities; their calmer counterparts they called Type B. Follow-up studies conducted at various research facilities supported these findings, and point to cynicism as a component of Type A behavior that is perhaps more damaging than others.[51]

Duke University researcher, Redford Williams, administered a section of the Minnesota Multiphasic Personality Inventory (MMPI) that measures hostility and cynicism to more than fifteen hundred patients being examined for arteriosclerotic symptoms. Those with high levels of cynical, complaining behavior were fifty percent more likely to have clogged arteries than those who scored low. The MMPI has been used extensively since the 1950s, and researchers consulted earlier test results which confirmed Williams's findings. One study of 255 physicians who took the test twenty-five years earlier showed that those with high cynicism scores had five times the level of heart disease as those who scored below the median.

At St. Luke's, we see a few patients who criticize everything. They feel upset with the world and do not appreciate any help they receive. Their selfishness damages not only them, but their families and friends as well. On the other hand, many patients of St. Luke's send warm thank-you notes after they visit. How their kindness refreshes us! We work hard to demonstrate our motto, Excellence With Love, and it's nice to know when we've succeeded. In their letters, people mention how much they enjoyed the natural beauty of the surroundings; and, always, they cite the staff—their soft voices, gentle touch, and caring attitude. These anti-cynics appreciate life and the people around them, so their days become a joy rather than drudgery.

Sometimes I wake up with a critical, cynical attitude, rather than a positive one of praise and adoration for the Lord. But I know I don't want to stay there. That's the key. What is the most important thing I can do in the early morning hours? Get rid of this poison. When I fall short, invariably it hinders my ability to love. My productivity at work also suffers. When I walk close to the Lord and surrender my cynical thoughts to Him, He changes my perspective and nurtures a beautiful, appreciative love between us that can flow to others around me during the day. This reminder in Philippians 4:8 keeps me on track:

> Finally, brethren, whatsoever things are true, whatsoever things are honest, whatsoever things are just, whatsoever things are pure, whatsoever things are lovely, whatsoever things are of good report; if there be any virtue, and if there be any praise, think on these things.

You Really Bug Me

In the *Peanuts* comic strip, Charlie Brown made the now famous statement, "I love humanity. It's people I can't stand." We can consider ourselves quite loving, as long as we don't have to deal one-on-one with anybody. People rub us the wrong way at times, don't they? The funny thing is that we do the same to them! We're just too self-centered to care.

No matter what our careers—whether as housewife, factory worker, or doctor—dealing with people on a day-by-day basis can test our love quotient to the utmost. Those in the medical profession face special challenges because patients only come to us with problems. Think about it. They rarely stop by when things are going well. (Of course, we wouldn't have time to see them if they did!) And if we doctors want to really sing the blues, we can go on about how exasperated we feel over government regulations, Medicare, the media, insurance, colleagues, lawyers…Little by little, daily frustrations can wear away our joy until we can no longer demonstrate a loving, peaceful spirit.

Some days when I'm feeling especially irritable, I have to remind myself how fortunate I am to be able to practice medicine. I can love and care for others and get paid for it! I try to offer specific thanks to the Lord for each patient I see and for each operation I perform. Neglect the discipline of this practice, and I revert back to my selfish ways in a hurry. Only by striving to maintain a heartfelt attitude of thankfulness and worship, have I even scratched the surface of real love. "In everything give thanks; for this is the will of God in Christ Jesus concerning you" (1 Thessalonians 5:18).

Ready to Blow

With minimal provocation, your blood is boiling. Cheeks flush, breath quickens, and muscles tense up. A verbal tirade chomps at the bit to storm the gate. We've all been in that situation numerous times, and regretted the aftermath. Proverbs 15:1 reminds us: "A gentle answer turns away wrath, but a harsh word stirs up anger" (NASB). We choose to ignore those words of wisdom.

Anger and temper often result from a self-centered mind that wants its own way and doesn't get it. Foul emotions, if left unmanaged, will damage their owner and all of his or her relationships.

Repressed anger can manifest itself as health problems—headaches, back pain, gastrointestinal disorders, and severe depression, to name a few possibilities. Temporarily disabling, they prevent us from producing our best to glorify God. Even the sanctioned, semi-controlled tantrums people engage in during athletic events do untold harm.

I have had a problem with anger. Because of it, I have struggled to experience the joy of the Lord. My temper has improved gradually—not through personal effort, but as I spent time with the Lord and drew near to Him. I simply threw up the white flag and asked Him to help me. The song, "He's Still Workin' On Me," describes my progress. But the Holy Spirit has cleansed me of my anger to a great extent. He'll do the same for you. If we're full of the pure Holy Spirit, toxic waste of spirit, mind, and body will have no opportunity to pile up.

One couple in our church celebrating their fiftieth wedding anniversary was asked, "What's your secret?"

They glanced at each other, smiled, and both answered, "Forgiveness. We never went to bed mad." Good advice from some experts, and Ephesians 4:26: "Let not the sun go down upon your wrath." We'll look more at the power of forgiveness in the next section.

Social Homicide

Hatred destroys! Like a rusty splinter allowed to fester in a wound to the point of severe infection, hatred intensifies as a result of long-standing anger. Jesus went so far as to label this form of self-exaltation "murder," a crime punishable by death in the Old Testament. Hatred wounds deeply, both the one to whom it is directed, and the one who carries it around inside. Such extreme unforgiveness corrodes our spirits until we can't love anyone. Worse yet, it can make us capable of acts of untold violence. We've seen proof of this in the increase in workplace murders by disgruntled former employees.

Hatred could have crippled me when I first started in private practice years ago. Let me share the story.

I was fortunate enough to know an optometrist who had been a high-ranking political official. He had a rare form of glaucoma. After I performed a successful operation on him, he sent letters of recommendation to the optometrists in the small town where I had relocated.

Now, in that same town, the ophthalmologists (M.D.s/ surgeons of the eye) had been rather antagonistic to the optometrists. I treated them all with equal respect, because it was the right thing to do. As a result, the optometrists— a group of professionals who had always been considered second-class citizens—sent many patients my way who needed a specialist. Success was inevitable with so many referrals. We used innovative techniques at our clinic, which added fuel to the fire. "It should take years to build a busy practice!" the others whispered among themselves. They gossiped, slandered, attacked, and made life very unpleasant. Some even resorted to outright sabotage. I struggled hard against a build-up of hatred inside me. Fortunately, God's forgiveness won over my base nature. For the most part, I maintained a peaceful attitude with the help of the Word of God and prayer.

In a hate-producing situation, simply doing for others is also good therapy. Responding with a servant's heart to those who have hurt us helps release us from negative emotions and personal rights.

> Let all bitterness, and wrath, and anger, and clamour, and evil speaking, be put away from you, with all malice: And be ye kind one to another, tenderhearted, forgiving one another, even as God for Christ's sake hath forgiven you.
>
> —Ephesians 4:31–32

A college co-ed was raped on campus by a young man and his friends. Understandably, for years she hated them for what they had done to her, until she accepted Jesus as her Savior. Amazing! She forgave them at last and even told them she loved them. God's powerful love, demonstrated through this young lady, conquered unforgiveness and the demonic powers of hell. "Hatred stirs up contentions, but love covers all transgressions" (Proverbs 10:12, AMP).

Forgiveness, one of the greatest characteristics of God, is so like Him and so unlike us. Without it, no man can experience the peace, love, and joy of being a Christian. Jesus personified forgiveness. As He was dying on the cross, He prayed for those who crucified Him, "Father, forgive them; for they know not what they do" (Luke 23:34). He enables us to follow His example as we rest in His love. He transforms us into spiritual overcomers. We need to ask for forgiveness from God and others over and over again. Hatred and God, like oil and water, don't mix. "If a man say, I love God, and hateth his brother, he is a liar: for he that loveth not his brother whom he hath seen, how can he love God whom he hath not seen?" (1 John 4:20).

PART FIVE

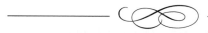

LOVE AT ITS FINEST:
OUR GOAL HELD HIGH

The highest love of all finds its fulfillment not in what it keeps, but in what it gives.[1]

—FR. ANDREWS, S.D.C.

Love for God is ecstatic, making us go out from ourselves; it does not allow the lover to belong any more to himself, but he belongs only to the Beloved.[2]

—ST. DIONYSIUS THE AREOPAGITE

To love and be loved, the wise would give all that for which alone the unwise live.[3]

—WALTER SAVAGE LANDOR

What must come first in all prayers, however varied they may be, and what gives them real value is the love with which they are made.[4]

—CHARLES DE FOUCAULD

Love at Its Finest: Our Goal Held High

REMEMBER MY CONVERSATION SOME THIRTY-ONE YEARS AGO with the kind, south-Georgia pastor? He surprised me with questions like "Why do you want to get married, Jim?" and "What do you mean by love?" I had the world by the tail... or so I thought. Marriage would be a piece of cake. And what newlywed doesn't believe that? (Just ask some of your friends to show you their wedding albums. See the euphoric expressions on their faces?)

Heather and I have learned so much since those early days. The good times, and yes, even the tough times, have taught us many things. Through it all, we've found genuine love to be rewarding, comforting, exhilarating, and sometimes excruciating *work* (that dirty four-letter word). Everything of value costs something to someone. Marriage is no exception. We get out of it what we put into it. Let me share a story to illustrate my point.

Imagine for a moment that you've been invited to a wedding. This one draws friends and family from near and far. The stunning bride, decked out in a fantastic gown, arrives at the sanctuary entrance on her father's arm. Her groom stands, quivering knees and all, at the altar. (He should quiver a little as he contemplates the magnitude of their decision.)

The beautiful ceremony goes according to plan: Scripture reading, music, pictures, candles, rings, *vows*. A limousine waits outside to drive them to the reception, and that, too, goes without a hitch.

Food, music, guests, fun, and more pictures. After spending the minimum amount of time with guests required by etiquette, the newlyweds wave their good-byes and zip away to begin their new life as husband and wife.

But what if, rather than heading off to a honeymoon together, they were to embrace, climb into separate cars (each one decorated with Just Married paraphernalia) and ride off in different directions? What if, from this point on, the two continue as if the ceremony changed nothing? They live in separate houses and have separate agendas. As time permits, they may correspond once in a while, but if they don't get a chance to write as often as they should, at least they call every few months. Sometimes that's the most they can manage. When someone questions their peculiar behavior, they admit, "Oh, we just wanted a wedding. We never intended to be husband and wife. Too much work. And besides, we're both so busy."

Ridiculous. People who marry intend to live together, to cherish each other, and get to know one another better every day. They want to become one, or at least think they do.

We all plan to do just that until the personal cost mounts after the honeymoon. We may never actually drive off to different destinations, other than for brief trips, but countless mates trudge through their days in mental, emotional, and spiritual isolation. Of course, engaged couples think their marriage will be the exception. Reality settles in soon after the fires of infatuation dwindle a bit.

Marital bliss doesn't happen overnight. It requires time and patience, but most of all, it requires a major change in attitude—a change from a preoccupation with self to a passion for the other person. Dare we do anything less than show God's grace to the one we vow to love until death?

God saves us by grace. We can't take an ounce of credit. (See Romans 3:24, 5:15, and Ephesians 2:5.) He cares about us as much as He does His own perfect Son. His love burns as strong for us now as it will in heaven when He transforms us from head to toe. We need only appropriate that truth into our hearts. That should leave us standing in awe. What magnificent, unmerited goodness He shows us!

In case we have questions about how far we should go in our expression of love for a beloved, God sets the standard for us. He sent Jesus. He gave Himself unto death for a reason—to wipe the slate clean between us and the Father.

The apostle John leaves no room for doubt about ultimate love. (See John 3:16 and 1 John 3:16.) It requires ultimate sacrifice, a readiness to lay down our most prized possession—our lives—for someone else, and not just someone who loves us back, either. An enemy! Outrageous. A commitment to God's will demands a willingness to go that far.

We cannot comprehend a love so intense. Would I offer my children to serve time in prison in someone else's place? Would you? God did more than that that for us! He offered His only Son to die for our salvation. The greatest human love shrinks to nothingness by comparison.

We can never add to what Jesus accomplished on the cross, but what if God does call on us to suffer or even die so that another can know Him? Have we considered that possibility? Are we ready? The blessing of martyrdom may never enter the picture for most of us. However, He does call us to love our family members at their grouchiest and whiniest moments. Essentially, we lay down our lives in love for another by giving up our "rights" to our own way and our personal comfort.

Peter, the apostle, overrated his personal devotion to Jesus. He thought he was ready to die with Jesus. Yet, when the pressure intensified on the night before Jesus' death and it threatened his own neck, Peter flunked the love test with flying colors. He denied three times, once with curses, that he ever knew Jesus. We'd best not look down our noses at our brother, Peter, though. How like him we are! Especially when we stand before the marriage altar in the presence of the living God, radiant in our wedding finery, making well-intended promises to love forever, under all conditions, an imperfect human being.

We, like Peter, vastly overestimate our strength of devotion. And so, like Peter, we end up flat on our faces, weeping, in the muck of failure. Enter, hope—Jesus of Nazareth! After His resurrection, Jesus reassured Peter in a very personal way that He forgave Him. He reinstated him in front of his peers.

He also asked Peter a pointed question, "Do you love me more than these?" using the word for self-sacrificing love—*agape*. Peter answered using the word *philia*, saying, "Yes, Lord, I love you as a friend." Jesus responded with an agape kind of directive, "Feed My lambs." In other words, "Show Me your love by caring for those I love."

Why did Jesus ask Peter three times if he loved Him? Jesus knew the answer without asking. I believe that, as a reminder that Peter had denied him three times, Christ now gave him opportunity to say before others that he loved the Lord—three times. Perhaps He was also giving Peter a chance to admit the truth: his helplessness to produce agape love in his own strength.

Only when we fully experience God's love can we accomplish one of the most difficult tasks we will ever be called to do—to love the unlovable. Jesus loved in that way when He walked the earth, and He does now. He loves prostitutes, lepers, the demon-possessed, and even murderers. With his agape love filling us, we will find it becomes supernaturally possible to love those who may not be very pleasant.

This kind of love reigns as the undisputed sign of a true Christian. In chapter thirteen of his first letter to the Corinthian church, Paul paints a clear picture of agape. As a powerful deterrent and stimulant, it hedges our way from wrongdoing and opens the door to righteousness. Colossians 3:14 admonishes, "And above all these things, put on charity, which is the bond of perfectness." The King James translation of *love* in these passages, "charity," loses impact on modern readers. Charity, to us, consists of an occasional donation to non-profit organizations. That does not scratch the surface of what true agape involves: a complete heart attitude and way of life.

First Corinthians 13 (NKJV) mentions nine characteristics of love:

- Patience: "Love suffers long"

- Kindness: "and is kind"

- Generosity: "love does not envy"

- Humility: "love does not parade itself, is not puffed up"

- Courtesy: "does not behave rudely"

- Unselfishness: "does not seek its own"

- Good Temper: "is not provoked"

- Guilelessness: "thinks no evil"

- Sincerity: "does not rejoice in iniquity, but rejoices in the truth"

Jesus' beloved disciple, John, described love beautifully in his first epistle. I offer it as our goal in life. The following passage from the Amplified Bible is rather long, I know, but before you decide to skip it, just try reading and meditating on it. Take it in bite-sized pieces, if you must. The Amplified version gives additional shades of meaning from the original Greek text:

> Beloved, let us love one another, for love is (springs) from God; and he who loves [his fellowmen] is begotten (born) of God and is coming [progressively] to know and understand God [to perceive and recognize and get a better and clearer knowledge of Him]. He who does not love has not become acquainted with God [does not and never did know Him], for God is love. In this the love of God was made manifest (displayed) where we are concerned: in that God sent His Son, the only begotten or unique [Son], into the world so that we might live through Him. In this is love: not that we loved God, but that He loved us and sent His Son to be the propitiation (the atoning sacrifice) for our sins. Beloved, if God loved us so [very much], we also ought to love one another. No man has at any time [yet] seen God. But if we love one another, God abides (lives and remains) in us and His love (that love which is essentially His) is brought to completion (to its full maturity, runs its full course, is perfected) in us! By this we come to know (perceive, recognize, and understand) that we abide (live and remain) in Him and He in us: because He has given (imparted) to us of His [Holy] Spirit. And [besides] we ourselves have seen (have deliberately and steadfastly contemplated) and bear witness that the Father has sent the Son [as the] Savior of the world. Anyone who confesses (acknowledges, owns) that Jesus

is the Son of God, God abides (lives, makes His home) in him and he [abides, lives, makes his home] in God. And we know (understand, recognize, are conscious of, by observation and by experience) and believe (adhere to and put faith in and rely on) the love God cherishes for us. God is love, and he who dwells and continues in love dwells and continues in God, and God dwells and continues in him. In this [union and communion with Him] love is brought to completion and attains perfection with us, that we may have confidence for the day of judgment [with assurance and boldness to face Him], because as He is, so are we in this world. There is no fear in love [dread does not exist], but full-grown (complete, perfect) love turns fear out of doors and expels every trace of terror! For fear brings with it the thought of punishment, and [so] he who is afraid has not reached the full maturity of love [is not yet grown into love's complete perfection]. We love Him, because He first loved us. If anyone says, I love God, and hates (detests, abominates) his brother [in Christ], he is a liar; for he who does not love his brother, whom he has seen, cannot love God, Whom he has not seen. And this command (charge, order, injunction) we have from Him: that he who loves God shall love his brother [believer] also.

—1 John 4:7–21

"How can I love like that?" you may ask. "I never could and never will."

Three cheers. The light of truth has dawned. Let's just be honest enough to admit it so we can open our hearts to the divine source of love and receive the help we need. How do imperfect, sinful, selfish folks like us ever love as God insists that we love? Before we answer this question in more depth, let me tell you an ancient legend.

One day, a wicked, ugly old man saw a beautiful young woman who captured his heart. Wanting to court her, he put on a Prince Charming mask. He portrayed the part so well that he won the maiden's hand. Five years after their marriage, a longtime enemy showed up on the scene who sought to destroy the image he had assumed. He snatched off the old man's disguise. To everyone's amazement, the face beneath the handsome mask was no longer that of a wretched old man. He had actually turned into Prince Charming!

In the spiritual world, masks don't work, of course. Religion has tried to get us to wear them for centuries, to no avail. There's no way to zap us from wretches into princes, fairy-tale style. We need that real gut-level transformation, from the inside out.

However, the lesson of the legend is that we do become what we commit to and focus on all the time. If we focus on Jesus, He conforms us to His likeness, which is love. If we focus on evil, we resemble it before long. The apostle Paul writes in 2 Corinthians 3:18, "But we all, with open face beholding as in a glass the glory of the Lord, are changed into the same image from glory to glory, even as by the Spirit of the Lord."

Marriage provides the consummate opportunity to tear off the masks and bring about an inner change from ugly to beautiful, from selfishness to the highest kind of love—commitment. A committed person will exhibit agape love. Commitment has a way of bringing us to submission under the Lord's direction as nothing else can.

Yet even a godly quality like commitment can become a tool for self-servitude. For example, people enter into a legal marriage, sanctioned by society, and are committed to expected cultural and religious beliefs. They say they love each other. In truth, after a short time, duty alone binds them together. They tolerate each other and cohabit...but love? No. The normal problems of life upset their fragile union and prove their lack of love. This counterfeit of true commitment rings false. It leads to a cold, dead marriage.

Why would mates refuse to appreciate each others' thoughts, passions, feelings, and dreams, yet vow through clenched teeth to hold the marriage together, no matter what? Why resign themselves to such a dismal fate? For any number of selfish reasons. Appearances. Convenience. Financial security. Fear of being alone. Fear of change.

No human ability can fulfill the marriage vow of commitment to love a spouse forever. Given bad breath, indigestion, and who knows how many other unpleasant occurrences of normal living, it's impossible for anyone to love another forever. Even commitment must be breathed on by the divine power of the Holy Spirit.

Over the long haul, only those things of the Spirit will last.

The wife who stands by her husband, without reservation, when he loses his job sets an example of commitment. The husband who remains faithful to his wife when she falls prey to a chronic illness does so also. These marriages have formed a bond not easily destroyed because Jesus Christ is the divine super glue in the middle. The author of Ecclesiastes knew the power of a God-centered marriage, as we see from his words: "And if one prevail against him, two shall withstand him; and a threefold cord is not quickly broken" (Ecclesiastes 4:12).

All good marriages possess a common, solid-gold core of commitment—first to God, then to each other. A fifty-year-old professional I know fell in love with a beautiful middle-aged lady. He faced a major challenge, as she suffered a partial handicap from multiple sclerosis. He married her, knowing full well that he would spend his life waiting on her. In time, she did become bedridden, but he continued to express selfless devotion toward her.

Even more amazing, a newspaper featured a story of a young couple who experienced an unbelievable crisis. On the first day of their island honeymoon, the new bride frolicked in the water. She was standing in a slight hole, so the water appeared deeper than it was.

Her husband plunged headlong into the water to join her. Snap! He broke his neck. In only seconds, their lives changed forever. Can you comprehend their devastation? Young, healthy, with dreams of the future, now facing quadriplegia. Many young women would have left, pronto. Not this young wife. She remained faithful to her husband. Today, they await the birth of a baby through artificial insemination, and they enjoy the deepest love possible.

As I was studying the theme of worship, I came across this poem. It describes commitment better than I can:

> Commitment is what transforms a promise into reality.
> It is the words that speak boldly of your intentions
> And the actions which speak louder than words.
> It is making the time...when there is none.
> Coming through time after time, year after year.
> Commitment is the stuff character is made of;
> The power to change the face of things.
> It is the daily triumph of integrity over skepticism.
> —Author unknown

Who was the greatest lover in the Bible, other than Jesus? Was it David? Solomon? Hosea, perhaps? Hosea wins my vote. That man showed undying commitment to his wife, Gomer, despite her blatant unfaithfulness to him. In many ways, we, like Gomer and Hosea, are tapestries of selfishness and selflessness. To the degree we imitate Hosea, we become true Christian lovers.

Ultimate commitment means ultimate love.

The level of forgiveness Hosea showed does not come easily, especially when it concerns a painful issue like an adulterous spouse. God put this story in His Word for a reason. It reminds us how much He loves and forgives us, and at the same time sets the example for us to follow. We have no right to expect perfection in our spouses. To do so only leads to misery.

As I see it, such commitment forms the backbone of Christian love. In fact, we could say that commitment is to love what the skeleton is to the human body. Although its somewhat ungainly appearance doesn't arouse many amorous feelings, where would a body be without the skeleton's strength and substance?

Such pure love exists only in God. We cannot conjure it up or duplicate it. Something wonderful happens when our spirit surrenders to His. An unfathomable love overflows to us. It activates commitment between any two of God's children who share a mutual faith in the Father's promises. God pours Himself into our hearts through the Holy Spirit (Romans 5:5), until our love for others conforms to His love for us.

In fact, dual forces act in concert to bring about this change in us from natural to supernatural love. The Holy Spirit acts as we seek Him to freely reign in us (James 4:5).

We come to realize that the Spirit must fill us and enable us to love others and serve them. Our commitment to seek the Spirit of God's help is the decisive commitment we make. He is able to produce fruit in us that is obviously the hand of God at work in us. "The fruit of the Spirit is love, joy, peace, longsuffering, kindness, goodness, faithfulness, gentleness, self-control" (Galatians 5:22–23, NKJV). As the Spirit works Christ-likeness in us, we are able to share the love of Christ with others, especially our wife or husband.

As a young Christian, and still very weak in the faith, I had much to learn about the Spirit-dependent life. Only with God's fulfilling presence in me could I accept His love, accept myself, love Him in turn, and be a vessel from which His love flowed to others.

If we don't know the Source of love very well, how can we express it? We can't. We must totally identify with Him to escape the destruction of our own selfish minds. As long as we are in control, we can't do away with ourselves. The Holy Spirit has to direct our love and empower our commitment before we can experience God's kind of love.

Even after all these years of walking with the Lord, I still like to think I can accomplish a whole lot more on my own than I actually can. I struggle to commit and submit myself wholeheartedly to Him, and so I struggle to love, even though the passionate longing to do so may be there. And I may very well accomplish a few things in my own strength, but the rewards don't last.

On the other hand, when God's love flows into my heart, it spreads peace and fulfillment within me. I delight in the Christian walk. I enjoy life. I want to serve others. Mere human passion can never do this. It teases and pleases for a while, then leaves us empty, craving more.

To become a reliable vessel through which God's love flows unrestrained, we have to first accept that love fully ourselves. Here's an example of that principle. In Central Florida, we have people born and raised in a southern climate, many of whom have never seen a single snowflake. They have never numbed their ungloved fingers on a snowball or felt the elation of skiing down a snow-covered hill in the crisp morning air. How well could they understand such experiences? How accurate could their instructions be about what to do in that kind of circumstance? Likewise, with love we must savor the taste of divine grace before we can demonstrate it to anyone else. Not only once at salvation, but every day.

Remember that beautiful passage about love from 1 John 4:7? "Love is from God; and everyone who loves is born of God and knows God" (NASB). That means if we would love as God intends for us to love, we must get to know Him intimately. He supplies the method and the means. We remain very much His passive instruments—plain old empty vessels holding His love and His Word, mixed together with prayer.

Just as friendships between people vary in their degree of intimacy, so do relationships with God. Most everyone claims to want closeness with Him, but few persevere in prayer and in the Word until they feel His presence. Most quit far short of what they say they would like to experience.

A hyperactive "self-life" stands somewhere between us and the fulfillment of our desire to know God. To develop intimacy—in any relationship, but especially with God—we must do away with our preoccupation with and protection of self. There's no other option. We must ask the Holy Spirit to fill us with agape from the top of our heads to the soles of our feet. Then, not only the things we say but the lives we live will bring glory to Him.

Ultimately, life presents us with countless choices every day. Most are so insignificant we may not even realize we've made conscious decisions, but we have. The process starts in the morning before we get out of bed. We all decide how we will love, live, and act. One of life's blessings involves our responsibility and privilege to choose between good and evil, between positive and negative mental attitudes. If we want love, we really have only one choice: to love Jesus Christ with all our hearts, souls, and minds. That's the million-dollar variable. Will we set aside enough time to become intimate companions of the omnipotent, living God, or will we settle for a pretentious interview with Him whenever we get in a pinch?

There's no secret formula for intimacy with the Lord.

We nurture this divine relationship by reading and meditating on the Word and spending time in prayer. He calls us to spend ample time with Him to speak to our hearts. During those precious moments when we're quiet before Him, the loving Master enfolds us in His tender embrace. He refreshes and renews.

Let's be honest: God cares less about the words we say, the titles we wear, or the works we do, than He does about our desire for intimacy with Him. Why? He knows if He takes first place, the rest will fall in line. That's why Jesus urged His followers, "Abide in Me and I in you" (John 15:4).

The Lord wants us just to sit still with Him awhile, to stay put and enjoy being in His presence. Abiding in Him implies a depth of closeness far beyond the hip-pocket prayers uttered on the run sometime between the moment our feet hit the floor and the time we dash madly out the door for work.

As children of God, we derive our strength from this abiding place. To put it another way, we need intense commitment to Him. We can acknowledge God, prefer God, have faith in God, worship God, have fellowship with Him and study His Word. But intimacy depends on all of this flowing from God's love received. As we drink in His love, the love of Christ for us will constrain or compel us to respond in surrender and obedience (2 Corinthians 5). The apostle Paul said he wanted to lay hold of Christ like Christ had laid hold of him (Philippians 3:12). For that to happen, our commitment to Christ is essential. But we must first trust in God's commitment to us. Our dedication is based in His dedication to us. We love Him because He first loved us (1 John 4:19).

Love, like a collage or tapestry, blends many disjointed aspects of life into a whole. The five kinds of love we mentioned at the beginning of the book (epithumia, eros, philia, storge, and agape) overlap and shift along the entire spectrum from utter selfishness to commitment. In other words, love ranges from one hundred percent taking to one hundred percent giving.

A golden thread of commitment winds its way through the tapestry of human relationships, strengthening and beautifying them for God's glory. It touches friends and family and fills moments of marital intimacy with divine satisfaction.

The opposite is also true, as much as I wish it weren't. Selfishness sneaks into everything good and spoils the design from above. Not even the most noble loves are safe from its influence. At any time, the relationship between two people can cross a fine line where selfish emotions spoil good intentions. If we're wise, we'll guard against such traps.

The cross of Calvary represents the world's worst sin: crucifying Jesus, the perfect Son of God. Thanks be to God that He transformed the greatest sin into the most monumental event in history. Because of Calvary, the worst selfishness of humanity was conquered so that as we accept Christ as Savior, we can become loving Christians.

Let's review several main points about love we have covered throughout the book:

1. We cannot love because we're too selfish.

2. Only God can truly love. He is love.

3. God's agape love must flow to and through us by His Holy Spirit.

4. For that to happen, we must get close to Him.

5. His Word and prayer become mandatory lifelines.

And the catalyst for all these interactions? Commitment. Dr. Stephen Olford defines that favorite word of mine this way: "faithful, fervent, and focused." Amen!

Love makes obedience a thing of joy!
To do the will of one we like to please
Is never hardship, though it tax our strength;
Each privilege of service love will seize!
Love makes us loyal, glad to do our go,
And eager to defend a name or cause;
Love takes the drudgery from common work,
And asks no rich reward or great applause.
Love gives us satisfaction in our task,
And wealth in learning lessons of the heart;
Love sheds a light of glory on our toil
And makes us humbly glad to have a part.
Love makes us choose to do the will of God,
To run His errands and proclaim His truth;
It gives our hearts an eager, lilting song;
Our feet shod with tireless wings of youth![5]

—HAZEL HARTWELL SIMON

EPILOGUE

ALL OF LIFE IS AN ENDLESS CYCLE. WE SEE SIGNS THROUGHOUT the universe: The sun rises and sets. The moon waxes and wanes, causing the tides to rise and fall on every ocean beach in the world. The stars, and their myriad constellations, are in a continual state of flux. Seasons come and go. Not even the huge glaciers of the frozen north remain static. All of humanity moves in cycles. We're born, grow up, mature, grow old, and die.

What kind of world would we have if newborn babies never developed physically beyond those first few moments outside the womb? It is hard to imagine. A generation or so later, there wouldn't be anyone to reproduce or care for others. It doesn't take a genius to see that this old earth wouldn't last long under those conditions. Yet spiritually a great number of us do just that. We never grow up.

The new birth is the beginning of an ultimate loving relationship with the Lord, but we must grow in it. Our relationship with the Lord is to be dynamic and exciting, a union that endures and matures. Commitment to God's will has challenged me to the utmost. It demands every ounce of discipline from me. As an avid participant in endurance sports, I can state without reservation that commitment to God's will is even more challenging than any endurance race

I have run. But it also gives greater rewards: it makes me a better spouse, lover, father, athlete, and doctor.

When we reach our golden years, the autumn of life, most of us realize that those things which once seemed so important really aren't at all. We attain a measure of wisdom. Of course, not everyone learns this invaluable lesson, but in the end, it doesn't matter. We have no choice but to relinquish our hold and release all we've received: youth, health, wealth, loved ones. Whether we do it willingly, or fight against the inevitable with all our might, the things of this world fade away. To experience the fullness of God's joy for us now, we must shift our focus from the temporal to the eternal—to God Himself, the essence of Love.

You know, this whole vast topic of love breaks down into three simple steps found in 1 John. Billy Graham's daughter, the fantastic Bible teacher Anne Graham Lotz, states them this way: "1) God's love for us; 2) Our love for God; 3) Our love for others. We need all three, in that order. Personalize those phrases now. Try saying to yourself, "God loves me. If I love God, I can love others."

In closing, I am reminded of the clever battery commercial starring two cartoon rabbit figures. They march along with batteries on their backs, beating their little bass drums. The first rabbit falls flat on his face early in the commercial. (Of course, he isn't equipped with the right brand.) "Bunny Two" sports the right battery, so he keeps on marching and marching and marching and marching...

That's us when we are plugged into God's battery. We keep on loving and serving and loving and serving...

Why not make a commitment to the real thing?

Natural love wears out; supernatural love endures.

Start today. Just love.

APPENDIX

The Beatitudes of Love

Blessed are those who find love everywhere, for they may never be lonely.

Blessed are those who always give love, for they shall always have more love to give.

Blessed are those who make it easier for others to love them, for they shall always have plenty of friends.

Blessed are those who always communicate in love, for they are channels of blessing wherever they go.

Blessed are those who bestow healing love, for they may be known as the physicians of the soul.

Blessed are those who leave love wherever they go, for the world will be a better place because they have lived.

Blessed are those who love to work, for theirs is the kingdom of service.

Blessed are those who love to share, for theirs is the kingdom of joy everywhere.

Blessed are those who love to wait, for theirs is the kingdom of patience.

Blessed are those who love to praise others, for theirs is the kingdom of appreciation.

Blessed are those who love to put others first, for theirs is the kingdom of humility.

Blessed are those who love to be courteous, for theirs is the kingdom of good manners.

Blessed are those who love God first, and above all, for theirs is the kingdom of right relationship to God, people and things.

Blessed are those who love Jesus Christ, for they share His tender compassion for the whole world.

Blessed are those who love and receive the Holy Spirit, for theirs is the kingdom of holiness.

Blessed are those who love what is right and good, for theirs is the kingdom of justice and mercy.

Blessed are those who practice love in relation to all people at all times, for theirs is the kingdom of intimate kindness.

Blessed are those who plan to practice love always, for they shall live in the house of love and dwell in the city of God forever and ever.[1]

—From *Forty Days of Love* by Thomas A. Carruth

How Important Is Love to God?

Eagerly pursue and seek to acquire [this] love.

—1 Corinthians 14:1, AMP

Whereas the object and purpose of our instruction and charge is love.

—1 Timothy 1:5, AMP

Pursue righteousness, faith, love.

—2 Timothy 2:22, NASB

Let love of the brethren continue.

—Hebrews 13:1, NASB

Love covers a multitude of sins.

—1 Peter 4:8, NASB

Love is from God.

—1 John 4:7, NASB

Keep yourselves in the love of God.

—Jude 21, NASB

He will quiet you with his love.

—Zephaniah 3:17, NIV

And above all these [put on] love...

—Colossians 3:14, AMP

He who has My commandments and keeps them is the one who loves Me; and he who loves Me will be loved by My Father, and I will love him and will disclose Myself to him.

—John 14:21, NASB

What Did Jesus Do and Ask Us to Do in Love?

I give you a new commandment—love one another as I have loved you. (See John 13:34)

Love your enemies, show kindness to those who hate you, bless those who curse you. Pray for those who insult you. (See Luke 6:27–28.)

If you love Me you will take my commands to heart. (See John 14:15.)

The Golden Rule of Love—Do to others whatever you would wish them to do to you. (See Matthew 7:12.)

Whenever you stand up to pray, forgive any grievance that you have against anyone; that your Father who is in Heaven also may forgive you your offenses. (See Mark 11:25.)

Then Jesus took some bread, and after saying the thanksgiving, broke it and gave it to them, with these words: "This is My body which is given for you; do this in remembrance of Me" (Luke 22:19, NKJV).

Father, forgive them; they do not know what they are doing. (See Luke 23:34.)

Be ready to make friends with your opponent. (See Matthew 5:25.)

If anyone strikes you on the right cheek, turn the other to him also. (See Matthew 5:39.)

If your brother does wrong, go to him and convince him of his fault when you and he are alone. (See Matthew 18:15.)

Scripture Meditations to Overcome Worry[2]

When we're anxious about a new situation and fear the unknown.

> So do not fear, for I am with you; do not be dismayed, for I am your God. I will strengthen you and help you; I will uphold you with my righteous right hand.
> —Isaiah 41:10, NIV

When we're anxious about our efforts to serve God and we feel useless and empty:

> So is my word that goes out of my mouth: It will not return to me empty, but will accomplish what I desire and achieve the purposes for which I sent it.
> —Isaiah 55:11, NIV

When we're anxious about the weaknesses we feel in our lives:

> My grace is sufficient for you, for my power is made perfect in weakness.
> —2 Corinthians 12:9, NIV

110

When we're anxious about decisions that will affect our future:

> I will instruct you and teach you in the way you should go; I will counsel you and watch over you.
>
> —Psalm 32:8, NIV

When we face opposition:

> If God is for us, who can be against us?
>
> —Romans 8:31, NIV

When we're anxious about the welfare of family and friends, we can remember that God is our Father and knows how to give good things to His children:

> If you, then, though you are evil, know how to give good gifts to your children, how much more will your Father in heaven give good gifts to those who ask him!
>
> —Matthew 7:11, NIV

When we're anxious about being sick:

> A righteous man may have many troubles, but the LORD delivers him from them all.
>
> —Psalm 34:19, NIV

When we're anxious about aging and getting old:

> Even to your old age and gray hairs I am he, I am he who will sustain you.
>
> —Isaiah 46:4, NIV

More Proverbs of Love

Your money is only as good as what you do with it.[3]

—John D. Rockefeller

A lovelorn porcupine was taking an evening stroll when he bumped into a cactus. "Is that you, sweetheart?" he asked tenderly.[4]

—Philip James Bailey

Don't marry the person you think you can live with; marry only the individual you think you can't live without.[5]

—Dr. James C. Dobson

Love is the fulfilling of the law.

—Paul, Romans 13:10

The Wedding Covenant

How does a covenant differ from a contract?

A covenant is based on trust between parties.

A contract is based on distrust.

A covenant is based on unlimited responsibility.

A contract is based on limited liability.

A covenant cannot be broken if new circumstances occur.

A contract can be voided by mutual consent.

What is the significance of a white runner in the aisle?

It is a symbol of walking on holy ground. A covenant is not made merely between two people and their witnesses. It is made in the presence of God, and He is actively involved in the agreement, since it is God who joins them together. (See Matthew 19:6.)

Why does the groom enter the sanctuary before the bride and make the vows first?

The groom signifies that he is the covenant initiator. This is important because whoever initiates the covenant assumes greater responsibility for seeing it fulfilled. God initiated covenants with Noah, Abraham, and David. Christ initiated the covenant of salvation with us. God is still at work to fulfill His covenants, and Christ will soon appear with the sound of trumpets to consummate the wedding with His bride, the Church. (See 1 Thessalonians 4:14–17.)

Why does the minister ask the question, "Who gives this woman to be married to this man?"

This question and its response symbolize not only the full blessing of the parents, but also the transfer of responsibility to the groom by the father. A daughter is under the authority and responsibility of her father until she is married. (See Numbers 30:4–8.)

Why do the bride and groom take each other's right hand during the wedding vows?

The open right hand offered by each party symbolizes their strength, resources, and purpose. By clasping each other's right hands, they are pledging these to each other. Just as we depend upon God for the "saving strength of His right hand," so each partner can depend upon all the resources that the other brings to the covenant relationship. (See Psalm 20:6.)

What is the real significance of the wedding rings?

In Scripture, the ring is a symbol of authority and the resources which go with it. (See Esther 8:2.) Also, whenever two parties made a covenant, they exchanged something of value as a token of their pledge. (See 1 Samuel 18:1–4.)

What is the purpose of introducing the new couple?

The introduction of the new couple establishes their change of names. In the marriage, the wife takes on the name of the husband, and the man becomes known as the husband of the wife. This name change is clearly illustrated in the covenant between Jehovah God and Abram. (See Genesis 17:4–5.)

Why does the couple sign wedding papers?

The couple signs wedding papers—a public document— to establish a public record of the covenant. God wrote out the testimony of His covenant in Scripture.

What is the significance of signing the guest book?

The guests become the official witnesses to the covenant. By signing their names they are saying, "I have witnessed the vows, and I will testify to the reality of this marriage." The witnesses can also serve as God's reminders to the couple to be faithful to their marriage vows.

Why is a special invitation given for the wedding?

The invitation for the wedding symbolizes the invitation to salvation. In the teaching ministry of Christ, He used the invitation to the wedding feast as an illustration of inviting people to partake of salvation. The wedding feast was free to the invited guests, just as salvation is free to all who will receive it. (See Isaiah 55:1.)

Why does the couple feed cake to each other?
This act symbolizes their becoming one flesh. By feeding cake to each other, they are saying, "This represents my body. As you eat it, I am becoming a part of you; and as I eat the cake that you give to me, you become a part of me." A New Testament illustration of this type of symbolism is in the Lord's Supper. Jesus took bread, broke it and gave it to His disciples, saying, "'Take, eat; this is my body, which is broken for you'...After the same manner also he took the cup..." (1 Corinthians 11:24–25). (See Matthew 26:26–27.)

BIBLIOGRAPHY

Bartlett, John, comp. *Familiar Quotations*, 10th ed., rev. and enl. by Haskell Dole. Boston: Little, Brown and Company, 1980.

Braude, Jacob M. *Speaker's Desk Book of Quips, Quotes and Anecdotes.* Saddle River, NJ: Prentice-Hall, Inc., 1963.

Dake, Finis Jennings. *Dake's Annotated Reference Bible.* Atlanta, GA: Dake Bible Sales, Inc., 1965.

Edwards, Jonathan. *Charity and Its Fruits.* Carlisle, PA: The Banner of Truth Trust, 1991.

Edwards, Judson. *What They Never Told Us About How to Get Along With Each Other.* Eugene, OR: Harvest House Publishers, Inc., 1991.

Friedman, M. and R. H. Roseman. *Type A Behavior and Your Heart.* New York: Knopf, 1974.

Hyder, O. Quentin. *A Christian's Handbook of Psychiatry.* New York: Fleming H. Revel Co., 1976.

Lewis, C. S. *The Four Loves.* New York: Harcourt, Inc., 1960.

McLellan, Vern. *Love Lines.* Eugene, OR: Harvest House Publishers, Inc., 1990.

Pepper, Margaret. *The Harper Religious and Inspirational Quotation Companion.* New York: Harper & Row Publishers, Inc., 1989.

Piaget, Jean. *Psychology of the Child.* New York: Basic Books, 1969.

Tan, Paul Lee. *Encyclopedia of 7,700 Illustrations.* Dallas: Bible Communications, Inc., 1991.

Vaughn, Ellen. *Radical Gratitude.* Grand Rapids, MI: Zondervan, 2005.

NOTES

Forequote

1. Quote from Web site: www.bestlovetips.com/html/love-quotes
   .html, accessed July 9, 2007.

2. Quote from Web site: www.quoteworld.org/quotes/8764,
   accessed July 9, 2007.

3. Quote from Web site: www.tondering.dk/maria/christ_q.txt,
   accessed July 9, 2007.

4. Quote from Web site: www.brainyquote.com/quotes/quotes/
   ssamlevenso392729.html, accessed June 26, 2007.

Prologue

1. Burt Bacharach, "What the World Needs Now Is Love."

Part 1—Love as We Know It: An Overview

1. Quote from Web site: www.cupidquotes.com/, accessed July 9,
   2007.

2. Quote from Web site: www.brainyquote.com/quotes/quotes/w/
   williambla150133.html, accessed July 9, 2007.

3. Quote from Web site: www.brainyquote.com/quotes/authors/m/
   mother_teresa.html, accessed July 9, 2007.

4. Quote from Web site: www.quaker.org/quest/issue7-2-nugent01
   .htm, accessed July 9, 2007.

5. Quote by Elaine Emans.

6. Quote from Web site: www.giga-usa.com/quotes/topics/love_
   t002.htm, accessed July 9, 2007.

7. Quote from Web site: www.brainyquote.com/quotes/authors/h/
   Helen_keller.html accessed on June 26, 2007.

8. Quote from Web site: www.brainyquote.com/quotes/quotes/b/ blaisepascl43456.html accessed on June 26, 2007.

9. Source unknown.

10. Quote by Heather Gills.

11. Quote from Web site: www.brainyquote.com/quotes/quotes/r/ robertbrow106539.html accessed on June 26, 2007.

12. Quote from Web site: www.brainyquote.com/quotes/quotes/t/ thomasjeff133002.html accessed on July 6, 2007.

13. *NETBible*, s.v. "epithumia," http://net.bible.org/strong.php?id=1939 (accessed February 4, 2007).

14. Fulvio Di Blasi, "Practical Syllogism, *Proairesis*, and the Virtues: Toward a Reconciliation of Virtue Ethics and Natural Law Ethics," *Thomas International*. http://www.thomasinternational.org/projects/step/essays/diblasi_000.htm.

15. *Eros* defined, found at http://en.wikipedia.org/wiki/Greek_words_for_love accessed on 1/12/07

16. *NETBible*, s.v. "philos," http://net.bible.org/strong.php?id=5384 (accessed on January 12, 2007).

17. *NETBible*, s.v. "philanthropos," http://net.bible.org/strong.php?id=5363 (accessed on January 12, 2007).

18. *Storge*, found at http://en.wikipedia.org/wiki/Greek_words_for_love accessed on 1/12/07

19. *NETBible*, s.v. "agape," http://net.bible.org/strong.php?id=25, accessed on January 12, 2007.

Part 2—Hindrances to Love: Selfishness, Pride, Worry

1. Andrew Murray, *Humility*, (Springdale, PA, Whitaker House, 1982), 83.

2. Author and source unknown.

3. Source unknown.

4. Quote from Web site: http://thinkexist.com/quotation/to_love_is_to_admire_with_the_heart-to_admire_is/191136.html, accessed July 9, 2007.

5. Quote from Web site: http://thinkexist.com/quotationrespect_
   is_what_we_owe-love-what_we/161294.html, accessed July 9,
   2007.

6. Webster's New Collegiate Dictionary, 9th ed., s.v. "selfishness."

7. W. Huitt and J. Hummel, "Piaget's Theory of Cognitive
   Development." *Educational Psychology Interactive.* http://chiron
   .valdosta.edu/whuitt/interact.html, accessed July 9, 2007.

8. St. Joseph's of Downer's Grove, s.v. "metanoia," www.stjosephdg
   .org/parish/about/metanoia.html, July 9, 2007.

9. Jonathan Edwards, *Charity and Its Fruits*, (Carlisle, PA: Banner
   of Truth, 1978).

10. Encyclopaedia Britannica Online, s.v. "hubris," http://www
    .britannica.com/eb/article-9041378 (accessed January 8, 2007).

11. Webster's New Collegiate Dictionary, 9th ed., s.v. "psychopathic
    personality."

12. Ellen Vaughn, *Radical Gratitude*, (Grand Rapids, MI:
    Zondervan, 2005), 66.

13. Ibid., 66-70.

14. Andrew Murray, *Humility*, (Springdale, PA: Whitaker House,
    1982), 5-6.

15. Ibid., 44.

16. Ellen Vaughn, *Radical Gratitude*, (Grand Rapids, MI:
    Zondervan, 2005), 29.

17. James P. Gills, *Rx for Worry*, (Lake Mary, FL: Creation House,
    2006), 5.

18. Ellen Vaughn, *Radical Gratitude*, (Grand Rapids, MI:
    Zondervan, 2005), 203.

Part 3—"Kinds" of Love: Understanding Relationships

1. Quote from Web site: www.brainyquote.com/quotes/quotes/m/
   mothertere131833.html, accessed on July 9, 2007.

2. Quote from Web site: www.best-love-quotes.com/great-love-
   quotes.htm, accessed on July 9, 2007.

3. Quote from Web site: www.theworld.com/obi/alt.quotations/
   Archive/fortune/love, accessed on July 9, 2007.

4. Quote from Web site: http://quotations.about.com/od/ lovequotes/a/lovequotes41.htm, accessed on July 9, 2007.

5. Quote from Web site: http://thinkexist.com/quotation/a_ successful_marriage_requires_falling_in_love/157722.html, accessed on July 9, 2007.

6. Quote from Web site: http://thinkexist.com/quotation there_is_ a_god_shaped_vacuum_in_the_heart_of/166425.html, accessed January 8, 2007.

7. C. S. Lewis, *The Four Loves* (New York: Harcourt, Brace, 1960), 1-15.

8. Ibid.

9. Ibid.

10. Ibid.

11. Ibid.

12. Ibid.

13. Ibid., 34.

14. Ibid.

15. Ibid., 35.

16. Ibid., 55.

17. Ibid., 59.

18. Ibid., 61–62.

19. Ibid., 91.

20. Ibid., 113–114.

21. Ibid., 94–95.

22. Ibid., 17.

23. Ibid.

24. Ibid., 98.

25. Ibid., 110.

26. Ibid., 111.

27. Jonathan Edwards, *A Treatise Concerning Religious Affections,* (Ames, IA: International Outreach, Inc., n.d.).

28. Ibid.

29. Ibid.

Part 4—*Love at its Worst: Selfishness Up Close*

1. John Piper, *What Jesus Demands from the World*, (Wheaton, IL: Crossway Books, 2006), 273.

2. Quote from Web site: http://thinkexist.com/quotation/love_is_the_master_key_which_opens_the_gates_of/7360.html, accessed on July 9, 2007.

3. Quote from Web site: www.brainyquote.com/quotes/quotes/m/martinluth110082.html, accessed on July 9, 2007.

4. Quote from Web site: www.brainyquote.com/quotes/quotes/h/henrydavid103440.html, accessed on July 9, 2007.

5. Quote from Web site: www.brainyquote.com/quotes/authors/m/marcel_proust.html, accessed on July 9, 2007.

6. Quote from Web site: www.brainyquote.com/quotes/quotes/t/thomaskemp121817.html, accessed on July 9, 2007.

7. Quote from Web site: http://hawaii.lib.overdrive.com/BFDF5C01-8BA9-49CF-9708-39681F9AC22A/10/199/en/ContentDetails.htm?ID=%7B1D629D9C-3EC6-46A9-8703-9C837D68228C%7D, accessed on July 9, 2007.

8. Quote from Web site: http://thinkexist.com/quotes/ross_parmenter/, accessed on July 9, 2007.

9. Quote from Web site: http://thinkexist.com/quotes/henry_drummond/, accessed on July 9, 2007.

10. Source unknown.

11. Quote from Web site: www.1-love-quotes.com/46709.htm, accessed on July 9, 2007.

12. Quote from Web site: , accessed on July 9, 2007.

13. Quote from Web site: www.brainyquote.com/quotes/quotes/c/charlesdic121823.html, accessed on July 9, 2007.

14. Quote from Web site: www.johnankerberg.com/Articles/_PDFArchives/practical-christianity, accessed on July 9, 2007.

15. Quote from Web site: www.christianitytoday.com/singles/eharmony/03oct-1.html, accessed on July 9, 2007.

16. Quote from Web site: www.brainyquote.com/quotes/quotes/w/williamlaw158260.html, accessed on July 9, 2007.

17. Allison Peers, Ed., *Ascent of Mount Carmel* (New York: Image Books/Random, 1958).

18. Source unknown.

19. Quote from Web site: www.brainyquote.com/quotes/authors/f/francois_de_la_rochefouca.html, accessed on July 9, 2007.

20. Quote from Web site: www.brainyquote.com/quotes/authors/k/katherine_anne_porter.html, accessed on July 9, 2007.

21. Quote from Web site: www.brainyquote.com/quotes/authors/s/sinclair_lewis.html, accessed on July 9, 2007.

22. Source unknown.

23. Quote from Web site: www.brainyquote.com/quotes/quotes/e/edmundwall198691.html, accessed on July 9, 2007.

24. Source unknown.

25. C. S. Lewis, *The Four Loves* (New York: Harcourt, Brace, 1960).

26. Quote from Web site: www.brainyquote.com/quotes/authors/h/henry_wadsworth_longfello.html, accessed on July 9, 2007.

27. Quote from Web site: www.brainyquote.com/quotes/quotes/a/alberteins148793.html, accessed on July 9, 2007.

28. Quote from Web site: http://quotations.about.com/od/lovequotes/a/lovequotes36.htm, accessed on July 9, 2007.

29. Sheila Cassidy, Prayer for Pilgrims (New York: Crossroad Publishing, 1982).

30. William Kingsland, Anthology of Mysticism and Mystical Philosophy (Whitefish, MT: Kessinger Publishing, 1997).

31. Alexander Robertson, Venetian Sermons Drawn from the History, Art, and Customs of Venice (Whitefish, MT: Kessinger Publishing, 2004).

32. Quote from Web site: www.brainyquote.com/quotes/quotes/r/robertbrow118373.html, accessed on July 9, 2007.

33. O. Quentin Hyder, *The Christian's Handbook of Psychiatry*.

34. John Piper, *What Jesus Demands from the World*, (Wheaton, IL: Crossway Books, 2006), 19.

35. Ibid.

36. Ibid., 23.

37. Ibid., 277.

38. James P. Gills, *Exceeding Gratitude for the Creator's Plan*, (Lake Mary, FL: Creation House, 2007), 157.

39. William Booth, accessed on the internet at HTTP://WWW.USS .SALVATIONARMY.ORG/USS/WWW_USS_EBC.NSF/ VW-SUBLINKS/41c746df0bf5610 ... 1/20/2007

40. *World of Biography*. s.v. "Mother Teresa," http://www .worldofbiography.com/0026-Mother%20Teresa/teach1.asp (accessed January 20, 2007).

41. John Piper, *What Jesus Demands from the World*, (Wheaton, IL: Crossway Books, 2006), 273.

42. Finis Jennings Dake, ed., *Dake's Annotated Reference Bible* (Atlanta, GA: Dake Bible Sales, 1963).

43. John Piper, *What Jesus Demands from the World*, (Wheaton, IL: Crossway Books, 2006), 272-273.

44. Ibid.

45. Quote from Web site: www.famous-quotes.com/author .php?aid=416, accessed on July 9, 2007.

46. Judson Edwards, *What They Never Told Us About How to Get Along With Each Other*, (Eugene, OR: Harvest House, 1991).

47. *NETBible*, s.v. "anechomai," http://net.bible.org/strong .php?id=430 (accessed on).

48. *NETBible*, s.v. "pistis," http://net.bible.org/strong.php?id=4102 (accessed on).

49. Webster's New Collegiate Dictionary, 9th ed., s.v. "cynic."

50. H. L. Mencken quote available at http://www.quotationspage. com/search.php3?Search=smells+flowers%2C+looks+around+ for+a+coffin&startsearch=Search&Author=&C=mgm&C= motivate&C=classic&C=coles&C=poorc&C=lindsly (accessed February 7, 2007).

51. Dr. Meyer Friedman, 1910-2001, accessed at http://en.wikipedia .org/wiki/Meyer_Friedman on 2/07/07.

Part 5—Love at Its Finest: Our Goal Held High

1. Quote from Web site: www.quotesandsayings.com/gpromise .htm, accessed on July 9, 2007.

2. Martin H. Manser, The Westminster Collection of Christian Quotations (Louisville, KY: Westminster John Knox Press, 2001).

3. John Forster, The Works and Life of Walter Savage Landor (London: Chapman and Hall, 1876).

4. Hanna Ward and Jennifer Wild, compilers, The Lion Christian Quotation Collection (Oxford, UK: Lion Publishing, 1999).

5. Source unknown.

Epilogue

1. Source unknown.

Appendix

1. Thomas A. Carruth, Forty Days of Love (self published, 1975).

2. James P. Gills, Rx for Worry: A Thankful Heart, (Lake Mary, FL: Creation House, 2007), 79–80.

3. Source unknown.

4. Source unknown.

5. Quote from Web site: http://thinkexist.com/quotationdon-t_ marry_the_person_you_think_you_can_live/202882.html, accessed on July 9, 2007.

About the Author

James P. Gills, M.D., received his medical degree from Duke University Medical Center in 1959. He served his ophthalmology residency at Wilmer Ophthalmological Institute of Johns Hopkins University from 1962–1965. Dr. Gills founded the St. Luke's Cataract and Laser Institute in Tarpon Springs, Florida, and has performed more cataract and lens implant surgeries than any other eye surgeon in the world. Since establishing his Florida practice in 1968, he has been firmly committed to embracing new technology and perfecting the latest cataract surgery techniques. In 1974, he became the first eye surgeon in the U.S. to dedicate his practice to cataract treatment through the use of intraocular lenses. Dr. Gills has been recognized in Florida and throughout the world for his professional accomplishments and personal commitment to helping others. He has been recognized by the readers of *Cataract & Refractive Surgery Today* as one of the top 50 cataract and refractive opinion leaders.

As a world-renowned ophthalmologist, Dr. Gills has received innumerable medical and educational awards. In 2005, he was especially honored to receive the Duke Medical Alumni Association's Humanitarian Award. In 2007, he was blessed with a particularly treasured double honor. Dr. Gills was elected to the Johns Hopkins Society of Scholars and was also selected to receive the Distinguished Medical Alumnus Award, the highest honor bestowed by Johns Hopkins School of Medicine. Dr. Gills thereby became the first physician in the country to receive high honors twice in two weeks from the prestigious Johns Hopkins University in Baltimore.

In the years 1994 through 2004, Dr. Gills was listed in *The Best Doctors in America*. As a clinical professor of ophthalmology at the University of South Florida, he was named one of the best Ophthalmologists in America in 1996 by ophthalmic academic leaders nationwide. He has served on the Board of Directors of the American College of Eye Surgeons, the Board of Visitors at Duke University Medical Center, and the Advisory Board of Wilmer Ophthalmological Institute at Johns Hopkins University. Listed in Marquis' *Who's Who in America*, Dr. Gills was Entrepreneur of the Year 1990 for the State of Florida, received the Tampa Bay Business Hall of Fame Award in 1993, and was given the Tampa Bay Ethics Award from the University of Tampa in 1995. In 1996, he was awarded the prestigious Innovators Award by his colleagues in the American Society of Cataract and Refractive Surgeons. In 2000, he was named Philanthropist of the Year by the National Society of Fundraising Executives, was presented with the Florida Enterprise Medal by the Merchants Association of Florida, was named Humanitarian of the Year by the Golda Meir/Kent Jewish Center in Clearwater, and was honored as Free Enterpriser of the Year by the Florida Council on Economic Education. In 2001, The Salvation Army presented Dr. Gills their prestigious "Others Award" in honor of his lifelong commitment to service and caring.

Virginia Polytechnic Institute, Dr. Gills' alma mater, presented their University Distinguished Achievement Award to him in 2003. In that same year, Dr. Gills was appointed by Governor Jeb Bush to the Board of Directors of the Florida Sports Foundation. In 2004, Dr. Gills was invited to join the prestigious Florida Council of 100, an advisory committee reporting directly to the governor on various aspects of

Florida's public policy affecting the quality of life and the economic well-being of all Floridians.

While Dr. Gills has many accomplishments and varied interests, his primary focus is to restore physical vision to patients and to bring spiritual enlightenment through his life. Guided by his strong and enduring faith in Jesus Christ, he seeks to encourage and comfort the patients who come to St. Luke's and to share his faith whenever possible. It was through sharing his insights with patients that he initially began writing on Christian topics. An avid student of the Bible for many years, he now has authored nineteen books on Christian living, with over eight million copies in print. With the exception of the Bible, Dr. Gills' books are the most widely requested books in the U.S. prison system. They have been supplied to over two thousand prisons and jails, including every death row facility in the nation. In addition, Dr. Gills has published more than 195 medical articles and has authored or coauthored ten medical reference textbooks. Six of those books were bestsellers at the American Academy of Ophthalmology annual meetings.

As an ultra-distance athlete, Dr. Gills participated in forty-six marathons, including eighteen Boston marathons and fourteen 100-mile mountain runs. In addition, he completed five Ironman Triathlons in Hawaii and holds the record for completing six Double Ironman Triathlons, each within the thirty-six hour maximum time frame. Dr. Gills has served on the National Board of Directors of the Fellowship of Christian Athletes and, in 1991, was the first recipient of their Tom Landry Award. A passionate athlete, surgeon, and scientist, Dr. Gills is also a member of the Explorers Club, a prestigious, multi-disciplinary society dedicated to advancing field research, scientific exploration, and the ideal that it is vital to preserve the instinct to explore.

Married in 1962, Dr. Gills and his wife, Heather, have raised two children, Shea and Pit. Shea Gills Grundy, a former attorney and now full-time mom, is a graduate of Vanderbilt University and Emory Law School. She and her husband, Shane Grundy, M.D., have four children: twins Maggie and Braddock, Jimmy, and Lily Grace. The Gills' son, J. Pit Gills, M.D., ophthalmologist, received his medical degree from Duke University Medical Center and, in 2001, joined the St. Luke's practice. "Dr. Pit" and his wife, Joy, have three children: Pitzer, Parker, and Stokes.

THE WRITINGS OF
JAMES P. GILLS, M.D.

A BIBLICAL ECONOMICS MANIFESTO (WITH RON H. NASH, PH.D.)
The best understanding of economics aligns with what the Bible teaches on the subject.
ISBN: 978-0-88419-871-0
E-book ISBN: 978-1-59979-925-4

BELIEVE AND REJOICE: CHANGED BY FAITH, FILLED WITH JOY
Observe how faith in God can let us see His heart of joy.
ISBN: 978-1-59979-169-2
E-book ISBN: 978-1-61638-727-3

COME UNTO ME: GOD'S CALL TO INTIMACY
Inspired by Dr. Gills' trip to Mt. Sinai, this book explores God's eternal desire for mankind to know Him intimately.
ISBN: 978-1-59185-214-8
E-book ISBN: 978-1-61638-728-0

DARWINISM UNDER THE MICROSCOPE: HOW RECENT SCIENTIFIC
EVIDENCE POINTS TO DIVINE DESIGN (WITH TOM WOODWARD, PH.D.)
Behold the wonder of it all! The facts glorify our Intelligent Creator!
ISBN: 978-0-88419-925-0
E-book ISBN: 978-1-59979-882-0

THE DYNAMICS OF WORSHIP
Designed to rekindle a passionate love for God, this book gives the *who, what, where, when, why,* and *how* of worship
ISBN: 978-1-59185-657-3
E-book ISBN: 978-1-61638-725-9

Exceeding Gratitude for the Creator's Plan: Discover the Life-Changing Dynamic of Appreciation

Standing in awe of the creation and being secure in the knowledge of our heavenly hope, the thankful believer abounds in appreciation for the Creator's wondrous plan.

ISBN: 978-1-59979-155-5
E-book ISBN: 978-1-61638-729-7

God's Prescription for Healing: Five Divine Gifts of Healing

Explore the wonders of healing by design, now and forevermore.

ISBN: 978-1-59185-286-5
E-book ISBN: 978-1-61638-730-3

Imaginations: More Than You Think

Focusing our thoughts will help us grow closer to God.

ISBN: 978-1-59185-609-2
E-book ISBN: 978-1-59979-883-7

Love: Fulfilling the Ultimate Quest

Enjoy a quick refresher course on the meaning and method of God's great gift.

ISBN: 978-1-59979-235-4
E-book ISBN: 978-1-61638-731-7

Overcoming Spiritual Blindness

Jesus + anything = nothing. Jesus + nothing = everything. Here is a book that will help you recognize the many facets of spiritual blindness as you seek to fulfill the Lord's plan for your life.

ISBN: 978-1-59185-607-8
E-book ISBN: 978-1-59979-884-4

Resting in His Redemption

We were created for communion with God. Discover how to rest in His redemption and enjoy a life of divine peace.

ISBN: 978-1-61638-349-7
E-book ISBN: 978-1-61638-425-8

Rx for Worry: A Thankful Heart

Trust your future to the God who is in eternal control.

ISBN: 978-1-59979-090-9
E-book ISBN: 978-1-59979-926-1

THE PRAYERFUL SPIRIT: PASSION FOR GOD, COMPASSION FOR PEOPLE

Dr. Gills tells how prayer has changed his life as well as the lives of patients and other doctors. It will change your life also!

ISBN: 978-1-59185-215-5
E-book ISBN: 978-1-61638-732-7

THE UNSEEN ESSENTIAL: A STORY FOR OUR TROUBLED TIMES... PART ONE

This compelling, contemporary novel portrays one man's transformation through the power of God's love.

ISBN: 978-1-59185-810-2
E-book ISBN: 978-1-59979-513-3

TENDER JOURNEY: A STORY FOR OUR TROUBLED TIMES... PART TWO

Be enriched by the popular sequel to *The Unseen Essential*.

ISBN: 978-1-59185-809-6
E-book ISBN: 978-1-59979-509-6

DID YOU ENJOY THIS BOOK?

We at Love Press would be pleased to hear from you if

Love: Fulfilling the Ultimate Quest

has had an effect in your life or the lives of your loved ones.

Send your letters to:
Love Press
P.O. Box 1608
Tarpon Springs, FL 34688-1608